Perfect Year 6 English practice from CGP!

At CGP, we love practice. We love practice so much, we even practised this sentence before writing it. That's why we've filled this book with more practice than you can shake a stick at.

There's a range of questions covering all the key topics for Year 6 English, including Writing, SPaG and Comprehension — all perfectly matched to the National Curriculum.

There are also progress tests throughout the book, to make sure pupils really know their stuff. Plus full answers included at the back!

What CGP is all about

Our sole aim here at CGP is to produce the highest quality books — carefully written, immaculately presented and dangerously close to being funny.

Then we work our socks off to get them out to you — at the cheapest possible prices.

Contents

Starter Test 2

Grammar, Punctuation and Spelling

Section One – Grammar

Nouns and Adjectives 6
Verbs and Adverbs 7
Synonyms and Antonyms 8
Pronouns 9
Clauses and Phrases 10
Prepositions and Determiners 11
Conjunctions 12
Present and Past Tense 13
Present and Past Progressive 14
The Perfect Form 15
Subject and Object 16
Passive and Active 17
Standard and Non-Standard English 18
Formal and Informal Language 19
Grammar Practice 20

Section Two – Punctuation

Sentence Punctuation 22
Commas in Lists 23
Commas After Subordinate Clauses 24
Commas After Fronted Adverbials 25
Commas for Extra Information 26
Commas to Avoid Ambiguity 27
Brackets and Dashes 28
Single Dashes 29
Hyphens and Bullet Points 30
Punctuating Speech 31
Apostrophes 32
Colons 34
Semi-Colons 35
Punctuation Practice 36

Section Three – Spelling

Prefixes 38
Words ending in 'shus' and 'shul' 40
Words ending in -ant and -ent 41
-ance, -ancy, -ence and -ency 42
-able, -ible, -ably and -ibly 43
Adding Suffixes to
words ending in -fer 44
'ei' and 'ie' words 45
Words with 'ough' in 46
Words with Silent Letters 47
Confusing Nouns and Verbs 48
Homophones 49
Spelling Practice 50

Progress Test 1 52

Section Four – Comprehension

The Titanic
(Non-fiction by Rebecca Greaves) 56
Letter by Serena Williams
(Non-fiction from The Guardian) 58
A Connecticut Yankee in King Arthur's Court
(Classic fiction by Mark Twain) 60
Poems about the Battle of Britain
(Poems by James Summersgill) 62
The Shapeshifter: Running the Risk
(Fiction by Ali Sparkes) 64
The Pool
(Poem by Andrew Fusek Peters) 66
Mary Shelley's Diary
(Non-fiction by Mary Shelley) 68
Interview with Quentin Blake
(Non-fiction from the British Library) 70
Who Needs Luck?
(Playscript by James Summersgill) 72
Yorimasa and the Monster
(Myth by Frederick Hadland Davis) 74
How to Cut a Pomegranate
(Poem by Imtiaz Dharker) 76
A Daughter of the Samurai
(Memoir by Etsu Inagaki Sugimoto) 78

Progress Test 2 80

Writing

Section Five – Drafting Your Work

Planning Your Writing 84
Editing Your Work 85
Proofreading Your Work 87

Section Six – Non-Fiction

Magical Mystery Tours
(Advert) 88
The Beautiful Game
(Explanation text) 90
Blue Whales
(Non-chronological report) 92
A King of the Past
(Newspaper article) 94
Letter to a Youth Group
(Letter) 96

Section Seven – Fiction

The Dragon Rider
(Fantasy story) 98
Far from Rome
(Historical story) 100
A Bumpy Ride
(Contemporary story) 102
Beneath the Stones
(Adventure story) 104
The Animals of the Rainforest
(Poetry) 106

End of Year Test 108
Glossary 114
Answers 116

Acknowledgements:

p. 58: Extract from an open letter by Serena Williams. Copyright Guardian News & Media Ltd 2021.

p. 64: Extract from *The Shapeshifter: Running the Risk* by Ali Sparkes. Copyright © Ali Sparkes 2007. Reproduced with permission of the Licensor through PLSclear.

p. 66: With thanks to Andrew Fusek Peters for permission to use his poem *The Pool*.

p. 70: Extract from an Interview with Quentin Blake, published 21 Feb 2020 © British Library Board.

p. 76: Poem 'How to Cut a Pomegranate' by Imtiaz Dharker from *The Terrorist at my Table* (Bloodaxe Books, 2006). Reproduced with permission of Bloodaxe Books www.bloodaxebooks.com.

p.108: Extract from *Tom's Midnight Garden* by Phillippa Pearce. Copyright © 1958 by Oxford University Press. Reproduced with permission of the Licensor through PLSclear.

A note for teachers, parents and caregivers
Just something to bear in mind if you're choosing further reading for Year 6 pupils — all the extracts in this book are suitable for children of this age, but we can't vouch for the full texts they're taken from, or other works by the same authors.

Published by CGP

Editors: Claire Boulter, Sian Butler, Tom Carney, Rebecca Greaves, Callum Lamb, Megan Pollard, Sam Summers, James Summersgill

With thanks to Andy Cashmore, Emma Crighton and Juliette Green for the proofreading.
With thanks to Emily Smith for the copyright research.

ISBN: 978 1 78908 779 6
Printed by W & G Baird Ltd, Antrim.

Text, design, layout and original illustrations
© Coordination Group Publications Ltd. (CGP) 2021
All rights reserved.

Photocopying this book is not permitted, even if you have a CLA licence.
Extra copies are available from CGP with next day delivery • 0800 1712 712 • www.cgpbooks.co.uk

Starter Test

Read the text, then answer the questions that follow.

Melusina's Secret

Hooves thundered across the forest floor. Birds started as he passed, scattering from the trees as quickly as meteors flash through the night sky. The count continued to ride, his sharp eyes watching carefully for a deer or boar hiding in the woods.

The count felt exhausted, drooping in the saddle like a wilted flower. He wanted to return home, but darkness was creeping in and he had lost his way. Suddenly, the air was pierced by a beautiful song. He stopped to listen. It came from the ruins of an old castle. He followed the voice, which was so bright and clear it seemed to light his way.

In the castle, beside a fountain, the count saw a woman singing. Her golden hair shimmered in the velvet light of dusk, and a white dress rippled like waves around her feet. She was the most enchanting woman he had ever seen, and the count fell in love with her immediately.

"Pray," he said, "tell me your name."

The lady's smile shone from her eyes. "I am Melusina."

Tripping over his words in his eagerness, he offered her his hand in marriage.

"You seem a worthy gentleman," she replied. She touched his armoured arm lightly. "I will marry you, but on one condition. When we are married, I will spend every Saturday alone, undisturbed, and on those days, you must never attempt to catch even a glimpse of me."

The count, marvelling at his wondrous fortune, readily agreed. At the prospect of a future with Melusina, all of his worries seemed to fade away. He helped Melusina onto his horse, and the two returned to his castle.

They were married, and for many years lived happily together, as much in love as the day that they had met. With her guidance, the count's lands prospered: the fields flourished, towns and cities blossomed, and he became known as a mighty leader. Through the years, Melusina also gave birth to a brigade of sons, the jewels in the couple's crowns.

Every Saturday, the count upheld his promise and Melusina stole away to spend the day by herself. This continued for many years, until one of the count's friends began to cast suspicion on how Melusina spent her time. Distrust sprouted in the count's mind, and the next Saturday, he tiptoed to Melusina's room.

The door was ajar, and through the crack of light, the count saw his wife in the bathtub: human from the waist up, but a tail, like that of a serpent or fish, had taken the place of her legs. As she splashed around in the water, he gasped.

Instantly, Melusina twisted around to meet his horrified gaze.

"Farewell," she cried. "You have failed me: this is the last time you will see me."

With an anguished howl, she transformed. Wings shot out of her back and she flew from the castle, vanishing forever.

Nobody saw Melusina again, but occasionally a mournful cry or the faint beating of wings was heard overhead as she returned to watch over her beloved sons.

Written by Siân Butler

Starter Test

1 Find and copy an example of a simile from lines 1-5.

....

1 mark

2 Suggest an adjective that could replace "enchanting" (line 10)?

....

1 mark

Why do you think the author has used the word "enchanting"?

....

....

1 mark

3 Give two ways that the count's life improved after he married Melusina.

....

....

2 marks

4 Do you think the count deserved a second chance? Explain your answer.

....

....

2 marks

5 How do you think the count felt after Melusina disappeared? Explain your answer using evidence from the text.

....

....

2 marks

Starter Test

6 Circle the adjectives and underline the adverbs in the following sentences.

The lake rippled calmly as the sun slowly sank beneath the distant horizon.

The tent we often use for camping is cosy, but uncomfortable.

6 marks

7 Add a pair of brackets to each sentence.

Allison who likes exercise is running a marathon in November.

The mountain which is difficult to climb is covered in snow.

2 marks

8 Circle the correct spelling of each word to complete the sentences below.

We made an agreement / agreemant to visit the treehouse on Friday.

The villain claimed that he was totally invincable / invincible .

Winning the talent show was a memorable / memorible event.

3 marks

9 Tick the sentences where the subordinate clause has been underlined.

Despite not knowing the way, I led the group onwards. ☐

Marcia's parents adopted a rabbit as it needed a home. ☐

All of the donkeys started braying while I was at the farm. ☐

2 marks

10 Rewrite each sentence using inverted commas and correct punctuation.

a raccoon is in my bin Frank shouted.

....

Isla moaned why did my umbrella break?

....

2 marks

Starter Test

11 Circle the description that best matches the ending below.

Jessie and Francis cowered in the shadows, trembling. There was no way for them to escape. With a devilish glint in his eye, the wizard raised his wand.

- Clear-cut
- Open

1 mark

12 Rewrite each sentence below using reported speech.

"I won't be scared if the volcano erupts," Leah said.

....

"The festival starts tomorrow," Jade told me.

....

2 marks

13 Match each piece of writing to the correct language technique.

- Thunder grumbled loudly overhead.
- The sheet of ice was a mirror.
- The cat's eyes sparkled like jewels.

- simile
- metaphor
- personification

3 marks

14 Write a rhetorical question and an exaggeration that could be included in the following advert.

Join us on Sal's Spectacular Safaris! Our amazing crew will drive you through our wonderful park, where you'll see animals thriving in their natural habitat. If you're looking for a fun, unique, exciting adventure, call our team and book a trip now!

....

....

2 marks

Score: ☐ /32

Section One — Grammar

Nouns and Adjectives

Warm Up Question

1 Circle the word that is <u>not</u> a noun or an adjective.

brave   be   teeth   horse

2 Rewrite these sentences, replacing the underlined nouns and adjectives with your own.

The <u>pizza</u> wouldn't fit in the <u>tiny</u> oven.

....

The <u>school</u> of <u>young</u> <u>fish</u> had never seen a shoe before.

....

The <u>sound</u> of <u>laughter</u> filled the <u>busy</u> <u>hall</u>.

....

3 Underline the concrete nouns and circle the abstract nouns in the passage below.

The crowd shouted with joy. There was a feeling of anticipation in the air. The singer walked onto the stage and began to sing the most beautiful song. Silence settled over the audience. When the tune finished, the singer waddled off the stage with great confidence.

4 Add your own adjectives to the sentence below. Use a different adjective each time.

Erica looked outside and saw a sky full of .... clouds and .... rain above the .... town where she lived.

5 Tick the sentences where the adjective is underlined.

The hilarious giraffe ran <u>quickly</u>. ☐   He bought an <u>expensive</u> teapot. ☐

We grew <u>beautiful</u> flowers. ☐   The flight was <u>very</u> long. ☐

Section One — Grammar

Verbs and Adverbs

1 Circle the correct form of each verb to finish these sentences.

Alex never speak / speaks and eat / eats at the same time.

I always loves / love visiting my friend's house, and I never want / wants to leave.

2 Using the pictures, write three sentences on the lines below, each containing one verb and one adverb.

1 ....

2 ....

3 ....

3 Underline the adverbs in these sentences.

Josh angrily snapped his pencil in half.

Maybe Chanti will win the top prize in the raffle.

Perhaps everyone found the film hard to understand.

4 Complete the sentences using the modal verbs below.

might   should   could

Alana wouldn't want a new bag, even if she .... afford one.

You .... really try the chocolate cake — it's delicious.

I .... start taking piano lessons, if I can find the time.

Now Try This Open a book on a random page and see how many verbs and adverbs you can find. Use some of them to make three new sentences that each have one verb and one adverb.

Section One — Grammar

Synonyms and Antonyms

Warm Up Question

1 Underline the pair of antonyms and circle the pair of synonyms.

hot / cold   complex / complicated   red / blue

2 Draw lines to match the words below that are antonyms.

3 Write a synonym on the dotted line for each word below.

strange → ....   easy → ....

huge → ....   scream → ....

funny → ....   scared → ....

brilliant → ....   leap → ....

furious → ....   gaze → ....

4 Complete the crossword with antonyms of the clues below.

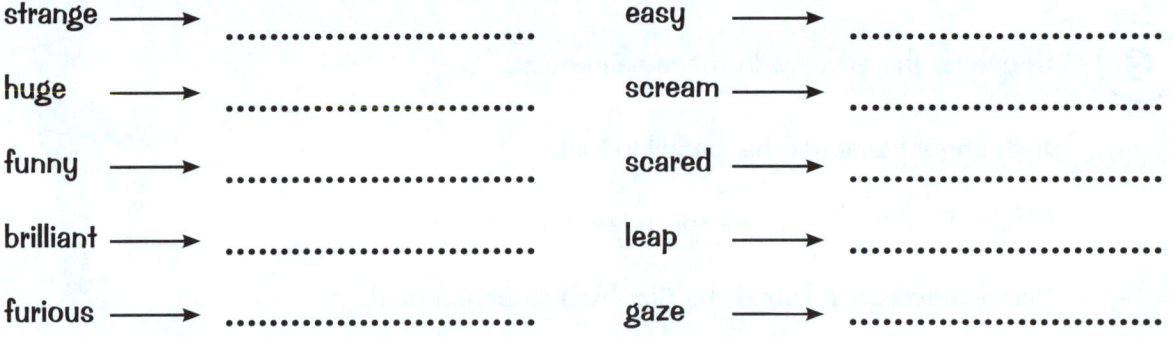

Across
1. wrong
4. bored
6. small
7. grow

Down
1. fall
2. short
3. hate
4. before
5. lie

Section One — Grammar

Pronouns

1 Tick the sentences that include a pronoun.

That idea was mine — don't copy me. ☐

The baby didn't play with the toy. ☐

Uncle Bob bought the beaver a bus ticket. ☐

Alice knew she had a good chance of winning. ☐

2 Use the pronouns in the box below to finish the story. Use each pronoun once.

| her | them | which | their | hers |

Words like 'which' and 'who' are relative pronouns.

Havva and .... little sister Ayse couldn't wait. First, ... dad bought the tickets and handed Havva .... Then, they saw an enormous roller coaster. The people on the ride screamed with joy — as they reached the top, all of .... let out a huge shriek .... echoed through the fairground.

3 Complete the story with pronouns from the wordsearch. Use each pronoun once.

My brother Rupert loves to destroy furniture. .... annoys my mum a lot. .... gets angry and calls .... lots of names. One time, he cut up a cushion .... was .... Later, she invited her friend Priya around, ... dog Nibbles helped Rupert tear down the curtains.

```
W H I C H Q Z
H T H I M F F
O H E R T U H
S T F L R F E
E Y X G X R R
S H E Y H G S
```

Think of five sentences. Each sentence should include a relative pronoun and one other pronoun. Make sure that you use a different pronoun and relative pronoun each time.

Section One — Grammar

Clauses and Phrases

1 Underline the subordinate clause in each sentence below.

When I was a pirate, I had a parrot called Gary.

Although I do not understand chess, I managed to beat my dad.

She speaks perfect French, even though she has never visited France.

If you start swimming now, you will reach Greenland by Christmas.

Luke always sang pop songs when he was alone.

2 Add a suitable relative clause to complete the sentences below.

The toddler, ..., wasn't great at darts.

I found a ladder, ..., and began to climb.

Tavan, ..., dived into the pool.

The shop, ..., was closed.

Annie begged her mum, ..., to buy a dog.

I saw the snow, ..., and jumped for joy.

3 Below are four expanded noun phrases.
Underline the preposition phrase within each one.

the scuba diver with her pet fish

a huge mountain near the lake

her favourite recipe from Greece

the beautiful fountain pen on the table

4 Expand each of the following noun phrases by adding a preposition phrase.

the nasty vampire ....

a long-lost necklace ....

 Think of three sentences describing your favourite fictional character.
Use a relative clause in each sentence. Make sure your sentences make sense.

Section One — Grammar

Prepositions and Determiners

Warm Up Question

1 Circle the preposition and underline the determiner below.

beneath   pale   those   stumble

2 Finish the sentences using prepositions that match the picture below. Use a different preposition each time.

The computer is .... the desk.

The keyboard is .... the printer.

The picture is .... the keyboard.

The chair is .... the desk.

The books are leaning .... the wall.

3 Use the determiners below to complete the sentences. Use each determiner once.

> many   their   these   few   which

This apple came from .... garden.

There are .... things I like less than broccoli.

There are some biscuits left, but there are aren't .... cakes left.

4 Write two sentences using the prepositions and determiners below.

> before   some   a

> because of   these   the

....

....

....

....

Section One — Grammar

Conjunctions

1 Circle the conjunctions in this passage.

Drew parked his scooter before he entered the ice cream shop. He had been here many times, yet the sight still took his breath away. The tubs of ice cream sparkled as the sun shone through the window. Although he was hungry, he wanted to keep staring forever, bathed in the window's glow.

2 Fill the gaps in this passage with the conjunctions in the box below to improve its cohesion. Only use each conjunction once.

> even though   because   so   but   and

I tried to put on a magic show for our class, ... it went terribly. I wanted to start with a card trick, ... I asked Michael to pick a card. Somehow, I managed to guess the wrong card, ... I did everything correctly. Then, I tried to pull my rabbit Tricksy out of my hat, but she was shy .... the whole class was giggling. She jumped out of my hat .... ran into the toilets.

3 Rewrite the passage below by adding suitable conjunctions to make it flow better.

It was a sunny day. We went on the school trip. We visited the harbour. I saw three porpoises playing. No one else saw them. I felt very lucky.

....

....

....

 'The cat left before dawn.' / 'The cat left before I could stop it.'
In which one of these sentences is 'before' a conjunction? Explain how you know.

Section One — Grammar

Present and Past Tense

Warm Up Question

1 Circle the verbs which are in the simple past tense.

ran   is   ate   went

2 Tick the sentences which are in the simple present tense.

The window cleaner visited my house.

The dog blew out the candle and wished for a bone.

My aunt sends me letters from Singapore.

Bobby leaves the house to go to school.

3 Circle the correct verb so that each sentence is in the simple past tense.

I <u>hopped</u> / <u>hop</u> to school on one foot because I lost a bet.

Shauna <u>wonders</u> / <u>wondered</u> what to do with her spare paint.

The bus <u>stops</u> / <u>stopped</u> in front of the castle.

Amrit <u>went</u> / <u>goes</u> to a golf club after school.

Andrew's bike tyre <u>burst</u> / <u>bursts</u> .

4 Write one simple present tense sentence and one simple past tense sentence about the picture below.

Simple present tense

....

Simple past tense

....

Section One — Grammar

Present and Past Progressive

1 Cross out the incorrect words to complete the sentences in the present progressive.

The architect (is / are / were) (draw / drawing / draws) a blueprint.

The scarecrow (was / are / is) (play / playing / played) a banjo.

I (were / am / was) (bake / baked / baking) a chocolate cake.

2 Write three sentences in the past progressive using the verbs and subjects below.

1 ....

2 ....

3 ....

3 Form the present and past progressive by using the correct form of 'to be' and the 'ing' form of each verb.

verb	present progressive	past progressive
to swim	Dolly .... alone.	Dolly .... alone.
to learn	The driver .... fast.	The driver .... fast.
to eat	Paula .... her meal.	Paula .... her meal.
to take	She .... the exam.	She .... the exam.
to think	I .... about sweets.	I .... about sweets.

 Using the past progressive, write three sentences about what you were doing last week, and three sentences about what you were doing last year.

Section One — Grammar

The Perfect Form

Warm Up Question

1 What form of the verb 'have' do you use to make the past perfect form? Circle one.

has   will have   had   having

2 Tick the sentences that are in the past perfect.

Anthony had no more water. ☐

Kasia has decided to bake her own birthday cake. ☐

The car had started to rust. ☐

I had used up all my ink. ☐

3 Write the past perfect form of the verbs in the boxes into each sentence.

Mrs Stevens .... her books.   (drop)

The taxi .... outside my house.   (park)

I .... the game at the last moment.   (win)

Arjun .... Adam's house before school.   (visit)

Misty .... a lot of marshmallows.   (eat)

4 Rewrite this passage using the present perfect form.

Eric opened his lunch box. Eric told his dad repeatedly that he doesn't like egg sandwiches, but his dad packed them anyway.

....

....

....

Section One — Grammar

Subject and Object

1 Complete each sentence by writing in a subject, an object or a verb.

(subject) .... fell asleep.

(object) Macy loves her new ....

(verb) The tiny dog .... at Finley.

(subject) .... stood on the sand, shouting at the ocean.

2 Circle the subject and underline the object in each of these sentences.

The air steward broke the chair.

The owl flies over the barn.

Two days ago, Aaron hosted a party.

Carys enjoyed the view from her room.

Kala bought a phone in town.

Satisfied, Talia ran home happily.

The shopkeeper closes his shop.

Will left his book at the beach.

3 Write three sentences, using a subject from the bag and an object from the case.

Bag: boy, frog, Kerry

Case: carrot, Ahmed, tadpole

1 ....

2 ....

3 ....

Now Try This — Write two sentences, each using all the words below.
Change the subject in each sentence: Timothy   drop   Rana

Section One — Grammar

Passive and Active

Warm Up Question

1 Circle the passive sentence and underline the active sentence.

The cat chased the string.   The string was chased by the cat.

2 Unscramble the words in each box to write a passive sentence.

(was ball The by Ali thrown)

....

(built table was Mum by The)

....

3 Underline all of the passive sentences in this passage.

The cinema was busy. Phoebe and Luca went to the counter and bought two tickets. They were asked if they wanted popcorn. They said no. The cinema was full of people. Luca was bored by the trailers. He started playing music out loud on his phone. Then he was told off by an usher. The lights went down and the movie began.

4 Rewrite each sentence, changing it from passive to active.

Jordan was thanked by Uncle Tim.

....

The match was won by Northstone FC.

....

The man was chased by the dog.

....

Section One — Grammar

Standard and Non-Standard English

1 In the boxes, write 'S' for the Standard English sentences and 'N' for the non-Standard English sentences.

I didn't see nothing. ☐   I could of helped you. ☐

Beth and Izzy haven't met before. ☐   Molly's done lots of paintings. ☐

2 Complete the sentences below using the Standard English verb form.

saw / seen   come / came   ain't / isn't

Raul .... you at the restaurant.

They .... to our house recently.

She .... going to play with us.

3 Draw lines to show whether each sentence uses a single negative or a double negative.

I won't sing no song.

I don't like that shirt at all.

Single negative

Chocolate won't do you no good.

Double negative

I can't find my books nowhere.

4 Write out each sentence below in Standard English.

They was losing in the first half, but then they scored.

....

I ain't seen Clare since Rachel and me went to her house.

....

"Have you seen them trains?"
Explain why it is non-Standard English to use 'them' in this sentence.

Section One — Grammar

Formal and Informal Language

Warm Up Question

1 Circle the most formal word in each pair.

father / dad   cash / money   get / receive

2 Rewrite the following informal sentences using more formal language.

I can't go to your birthday party because I've got a family thing.

....

I'm feeling pretty under the weather, to be honest.

....

She's a famous footballer, isn't she?

....

3 Tick each sentence that uses the subjunctive form.

You knew the answer, but you wouldn't tell me. ☐

Ricardo would never do something like that. ☐

It is crucial that you be awake at all times. ☐

If I were the Queen, I would abolish Mondays. ☐

4 Circle the correct words to complete the sentences in the subjunctive form.

If I was / were alone, I would read a book.

She proposes that you write / wrote the play.

It is essential that the class is / be quiet during this presentation.

I wouldn't eat that if I were / was you.

The King insists that all swords be / are sheathed immediately.

Section One — Grammar

Grammar Practice

Warm Up Question

1 Add a noun and adjective to each sentence below.

The .... is ....   The .... looked ....

2 Use the correct pronouns to complete this extract.

I went out to see the night sky with my older brother. Astronomy is his hobby — .... knows a lot about planets and stars. We climbed to the top of a hill. I didn't have a telescope so he let me use .... Suddenly, another stargazer shouted. .... could see Jupiter in her telescope. .... all took turns to look and it was amazing.

3 Write a synonym and an antonym for each word below.

	danger	perfect	skilful
synonym	....	....	....
antonym	....	....	....

4 Use co-ordinating conjunctions to form two sentences from the clauses below.

(I was tired)   (Chloe likes pears)   (I lay down)   (she hates apples)

1 ....

2 ....

5 Write 'M' for main clause or 'R' for relative clause next to the clauses underlined below.

Danielle, <u>who was afraid of the dark</u>, kept her night light on.   ☐

<u>They discovered the mouse</u> that had been eating all of the flour.   ☐

The tennis stadium, <u>which was open-air</u>, was flooded by the rain.   ☐

Section One — Grammar

Grammar Practice

6 Circle the correct option so that each sentence is in Standard English.

We was / were there last year, and we saw / seen Lydia's family.

You should have / of asked who did / done it.

My cousins was / were in the shop but they didn't see nothing / anything .

7 Draw lines to match each sentence to the correct form.

Dad cooks fish fingers on Fridays. past progressive

I have seen that film twice. simple present

I had just discovered a treasure map. past perfect

This time last year, we were exploring Mexico City. present perfect

8 Unscramble the words below to make a sentence that uses the subjunctive form.

requests at The head teacher meeting that parents present the be

....

....

9 Rewrite the sentences below in the active voice.

A game of football was played by my team. A goal was scored by me.

....

....

Now Try This Starting with your answer to question 9, write two paragraphs of a short story using the simple past tense and the simple present tense.

Section Two — Punctuation

Sentence Punctuation

Warm Up Questions

1. Give one reason why you might use a capital letter. ....

2. True or false? Exclamation marks are only used at the end of a command. ....

3. Tick the sentence that uses capital letters and full stops correctly.

   I wanted to go to the zoo but William didn't. ☐

   My friend Ibrahim wants to be a vet when he grows up ☐

   Sarah and Joe like visiting their aunt in portugal. ☐

4. Circle the words in each sentence that should have a capital letter.

   alec had two guinea pigs called popcorn and scrapper.

   padma is going to stay in cornwall next march.

5. Draw lines to match each sentence to the correct punctuation mark.

   Do you like apples   !   Don't sit there

   That's incredible   Shall we ride our bikes

   This film is terrifying   ?   Have you seen my sock

6. Write a sentence that ends with the punctuation shown.

   [?] ....

   [!] ....

Commas in Lists

1 Tick the sentences that use commas correctly.

Danny took a camera, a notebook, and a pencil on the walk. ☐

Hannah's best friends are called Meena, Tina and Sabrina. ☐

I swung, on the swing climbed on the climbing frame and zipped down the zip wire. ☐

Timon has posters of pop stars, footballers and dragons on his wall. ☐

I'm wearing purple, trainers red jeans, a green top and a yellow hat. ☐

2 Add commas in the correct places in the sentences below.

The octopus had many legs a hat and a worried look.

My sister likes football hockey swimming and running.

Jess had a party with lots of games a magician and a bouncy castle.

Nadia's three brothers are called Hari Umar and Malik.

I got two board games three books and some chocolate for Christmas.

3 Write a list of four things to complete each sentence. Remember to use commas in the correct places.

My favourite hobbies are ....

....

My best friend has ....

....

I would like to visit ....

....

Now Try This Write a short paragraph about what you did last weekend. Make sure that you include at least two lists of three things or more. Remember to use commas correctly.

Section Two — Punctuation

Commas After Subordinate Clauses

1 Tick the sentences that use commas correctly.

Because he was bored Marcus tried, on all the hats. ☐

Although Kim enjoys swimming, she doesn't like the sea. ☐

When I am older, I'll write a book about my life. ☐

After we have eaten, dinner we'll have ice cream. ☐

2 Add commas in the correct places in the sentences below.

Although she's small Harriet's very good at basketball.

Before we go home let's go to the park.

When their dad arrived Mo and Kit hid in the bushes.

After 'Talented Elephants' finishes we'll watch 'Dogs Ahoy'.

3 Match the subordinate clause to the correct main clause. Then write out the complete sentences with commas in the correct places.

Until the food arrives — Samara stayed up late.

As she was on holiday — I will be hungry.

Unless you like cats — you shouldn't go there.

....

....

....

 Write three sentences that each start with a different subordinate clause. Remember to use a comma in the correct place in each sentence.

Section Two — Punctuation

Commas After Fronted Adverbials

Warm Up Question

1 Underline the sentence that has a comma in the correct place.

In September we are going, to Florida.

In September, we are going to Florida.

2 Write these sentences on the lines, adding in commas where they are needed.

Twice a week I play tiddlywinks.

....

At the back of the drawer you'll find the forks.

....

After an hour Suzie went home.

....

3 Add commas in the correct places in the sentences below.

In Spain we went windsurfing three times.

With a cackle of glee the witch vanished.

Before dinner Rowan went for a bike ride.

On Tuesday afternoon we're going skating.

Last night Zoe read a book in her armchair.

4 Complete the sentences below by adding main clauses. Remember to put commas in the correct places.

Next year ....

On Saturday mornings ....

At the end of the road ....

In London ....

Commas For Extra Information

1 Tick the sentences that use commas correctly.

The pigsty, which is next to the stable, always smells bad. ☐

My favourite, band Rainbow Sparks, are playing here next month. ☐

Pascal's uncle, who lives in Argentina sent me, a postcard. ☐

I like all animals, even spiders, but bats are my favourite. ☐

2 Rewrite the sentences below, adding the extra information in the boxes. Use commas where they are needed.

Josh helped me reach the book.   (who's very tall)

....

Ama is coming over soon.   (my new friend)

....

Our house makes strange noises.   (the oldest on the street)

....

3 Add commas in the correct places in the passage below.

Last Monday which was very warm and sunny we went to the beach. We travelled on a double-decker bus which was orange for over an hour. Ben my best friend fell asleep on the bus. Ben and I built a sculpture a huge turtle out of sand on the beach. Ella who is very generous let us eat some of her biscuits at lunchtime. When we got home late that afternoon we were tired but happy.

Now Try This Find three short sentences in a book or magazine and rewrite them, adding in extra information. Remember to add a comma either side of the information you add.

Section Two — Punctuation

Commas to Avoid Ambiguity

Warm Up Question

1 Draw lines to match each sentence to the correct meaning.

What time do you want to eat Fluffy?   Asking what time Fluffy wants to eat.

What time do you want to eat, Fluffy?   Asking what time you want to eat Fluffy.

2 Rewrite the sentences, adding in a comma to change their meaning.

I bought chocolate biscuits and cake.

....

After watching Olly, Ian and Paul went home.

....

We decided to clean up Rufus.

....

Most of the time travellers forget to bring a toothbrush.

....

3 Add a comma to each sentence below to change its meaning.

Hubert liked cream cakes and cherries.

My best friends are Kiana Albert and Doug.

I invited my sisters, Patsy and Lizzie for dinner.

4 Read the two sentences below. Explain how the meaning of the sentence changes when the comma is moved.

Not wanting to wake up Gwen, Ashley lay quietly.

Not wanting to wake up, Gwen Ashley lay quietly.

....

....

....

Brackets and Dashes

Warm Up Question

1 Underline the sentence that uses brackets correctly.

Jill (my cousin) has a pet snake.   Jill my cousin has (a pet snake).

2 Add a pair of brackets in the correct place in the sentences below.

Mrs Higgins our next-door neighbour has six cats .

Hassan is going to the bookshop the one near his house .

Our Christmas party the one at school didn't go according to plan .

3 Complete each sentence by writing something in the gaps between the brackets.

Percy (..) lent me his bike.

My friend (..) moved to a new house.

4 Each of these sentences needs a pair of dashes. Put them into the correct boxes.

My brother ☐ who is in the army ☐ is staying ☐ with us.

Darla met ☐ a trapeze artist ☐ Madame Volero ☐ at the circus.

Asa's kite ☐ the bright ☐ red one ☐ got stuck ☐ in a tree.

5 Rewrite each of these sentences in the correct order using a pair of dashes.

| Hardi's house | is very big | the one with the green door |

....

| is coming to visit | my aunt | who lives in Brighton |

....

Section Two — Punctuation

Single Dashes

1 Tick the sentences that use a dash correctly.

I went for a run — I wanted to get fit. ☐

Gemma ate — her dinner really quickly. ☐

Simon told me his secret — he didn't like cheese. ☐

We all enjoyed the fairground — last night. ☐

2 Each of these sentences needs a single dash. Put the dashes into the correct boxes.

I ☐ couldn't believe it ☐ we saw a rare spotted ☐ wallaby.

I needed ☐ some new socks ☐ the old ones ☐ had holes in.

Sean told his pig ☐ off ☐ it had eaten ☐ all the pizza.

3 Only one of the dashes is needed in each of these sentences. Cross out all the dashes that aren't needed.

We were worried — we couldn't find our dog — Lucky anywhere.

I had that dream — again last night — the one about pirates.

Don't touch — that button — you don't know what — it does.

Wen Yu climbed — the tree — he wanted to see — the view.

4 Complete each sentence by using a dash to separate two clauses.

Mr Assad looked over the fence ....

We went into town ....

Now Try This

Why does the following sentence use a dash and not a comma?

'Miko was thirsty — she had been playing badminton for two hours.'

Section Two — Punctuation

Hyphens and Bullet Points

Warm Up Question

1 Circle the phrase that uses hyphens correctly.

blue eyed-sheep   blue eyed sheep   blue-eyed sheep   blue-eyed-sheep

2 Tick the sentences that use hyphens correctly.

My basketball-mad sister is always practising. ☐

We travelled to far flung places and exotic-lands. ☐

Tariq described himself as a self made-man. ☐

Serena lives in a high-rise apartment building. ☐

3 Circle the correct word to complete the sentences so they make sense.

I had to re-mark / remark the lines of the hockey pitch after it rained.

Shana recapped / re-capped the plot of the thriller for her mum.

At school, we re-cycle / recycle all our scrap paper.

I decided to return / re-turn the new bike wheel when I realised it was bent.

4 Write out this passage as a list using bullet points.

Cut out the shape you want your mask to be. Decorate your mask using whatever materials you have. Use a sharp pencil to make a hole on either side. Thread elastic through the holes and tie a knot in each end.

To make a mask, follow these steps:

....

....

....

....

Section Two — Punctuation

Punctuating Speech

1 Fill in the boxes with the correct punctuation to complete each sentence.

"Look where you're going! ▢ my brother shouted as I tripped over his model ▢

Tracey called to me, ▢ Do you want to come over for tea tonight? ▢

"It's the best present ever ▢ ▢ Jamal yelled excitedly.

Jed asked me ▢ "Can I go on your trampoline ▢ ▢

"I'll come too ▢ ▢ said Polly ▢ "since it was my idea."

"Shall we watch TV? ▢ Sam asked ▢ "What do you want to do ▢ "

2 Punctuate these sentences with inverted commas, full stops and commas.

I can't find my toothbrush anywhere Mum called

Olly said I think I'll go swimming tonight

I'm sure I will find a cure for all illness said Lauren

I'm not sleepy said Chris so I think I'll stay up longer

Kell can't come said Gemma but Nathan can

3 Use the words on each postcard to write a sentence that includes inverted commas.

asked | banana
want | Meg

....
....

teapot | said
have | Jonah

....
....

 Write out a short conversation between two of the characters from your favourite book or TV show. Think carefully about how the speech should be punctuated.

Apostrophes

Warm Up Questions

1 Shorten these words using apostrophes.

I will ....   you are ....   it is ....

2 Underline the sentence that uses apostrophes correctly.

We walked Laura's dog.   We walked Lauras' dog.

3 Rewrite each sentence below. Change the underlined words into their contracted forms using an apostrophe.

<u>I am</u> going home now.

....

<u>We are</u> going to do what he says.

....

<u>I had</u> been expecting that <u>it would</u> do that.

....

4 Rewrite each of these contracted forms as its longer version.

he'll ....   you've ....

won't ....   couldn't ....

5 Write the words in the boxes into each sentence in their contracted form.

Peri .... enjoyed this if she had come.   [would have]

I .... know you lived here.   [did not]

"........................... my pen?" asked Milo.   [Where is]

Section Two — Punctuation

Apostrophes

6 Circle the correct word to complete the sentences so that they make sense.

We're all going to Jamies' / Jamie's house for a sleepover.

The glasses' / glass's rims were all chipped.

Farah's / Farahs' tongue went blue after she ate the lolly.

That drummers' / drummer's hands are moving really quickly.

Both farmers' / farmer's pigs escaped that summer.

The children's / childrens' parents looked tired.

The donkey's / donkeys' leg was really hairy.

7 Write a sentence about each set of words, using an apostrophe to show possession.

Ellie   shirt   purple   ....

cat   tail   fluffy   ....

mouse   ear   twitch   ....

pandas   cubs   play   ....

buses   tyres   flat   ....

8 Write 'its' or 'it's' to complete the sentences below.

The eagle spread .... wings.   Wow, ... really nice in here.

I hope .... not too hot.   This gum has lost .... flavour.

I wonder if .... raining.   .... my birthday today.

The boat had lost .... oars.   The cow curled around .... calf.

Now Try This Write out a short paragraph about a school trip. Use all of the following: a contracted form, an apostrophe for possession, 'its' and 'it's'.

Section Two — Punctuation

Colons

Warm Up Question

1 Circle the one correct colon in each sentence below.

I have lots of hobbies : reading , playing guitar , judo : and collecting shells .

Zara didn't want : to go to the park : she had been there yesterday .

2 Tick the sentences that use colons correctly.

I'd like three things: a new bike, some chocolate and a time machine. ☐

Tom visited several: countries Thailand, Laos and Vietnam. ☐

I wish I could talk to animals: I'd like to know what my cat is thinking. ☐

Jon doesn't like: parsnips he thinks they're too sweet. ☐

The room was bright: all the lights were on. ☐

3 Add colons in the correct places in these sentences.

Stan collected what he needed to paint a picture paints, paper and brushes.

Aisha went swimming she needed to cool down.

Aaron didn't want to go home he was having too much fun.

The otter could do tricks diving, catching fish and waving.

Caitlyn turned on the radio she wanted to hear her favourite show.

I took three things on holiday my passport, some money and a book.

4 Write a sentence about the picture below which includes a colon.

....

....

Section Two — Punctuation

Semi-Colons

1 Tick the sentences where a semi-colon could be used instead of the conjunction.

My favourite subject is art <u>and</u> my least favourite is maths. ☐

We could play a board game <u>or</u> watch a film. ☐

Cora likes going to Iceland <u>but</u> I prefer Spain. ☐

I was really bored <u>so</u> I decided to dress up my cat, Gavin. ☐

2 Each of these sentences is missing two semi-colons. Put them into the correct boxes.

In Paris, I want to visit ☐ the Louvre, a famous art gallery ☐ the Eiffel Tower, the tallest structure ☐ in the city ☐ and the shops, which are world-renowned.

Nat was planning ☐ a special meal ☐ for Beth, including salmon, ☐ caught that day ☐ peas, fresh from the garden ☐ and tiramisu, Beth's favourite.

During the summer, we ☐ went paddle boarding, which I've always wanted ☐ to try ☐ sailing, which was fun ☐ and paintballing, although ☐ I didn't like that.

3 Rewrite the passage below, adding semi-colons in the correct places.

We decided to go stargazing Mel stayed at home. We saw the Milky Way, like a long white cloud a meteor, which fell really fast and Mars, which was a pinkish colour.

....

....

....

Now Try This For each of the following, think of a clause that could be added after the semi-colon:
Ezra likes dogs; I bought birdseed; Kit opened the box; Jan read a book;

Section Two — Punctuation

Punctuation Practice

Warm Up Question

1 Circle the most suitable punctuation mark to complete these sentences.

Do you want some melon   .   ?   !   I think we should go for a walk   .   ?   !

What a wonderful day   .   ?   !   Shall I ask Carrie to come   .   ?   !

2 Add commas in the correct places in the sentences below.

Last week we saw fourteen ducklings.

We decorated the table with candles flowers and confetti.

After Lee had ridden the dragon he needed to sit down.

Above Karen's head a large flock of geese circled.

I need to take the ingredients an apron and my cookbook.

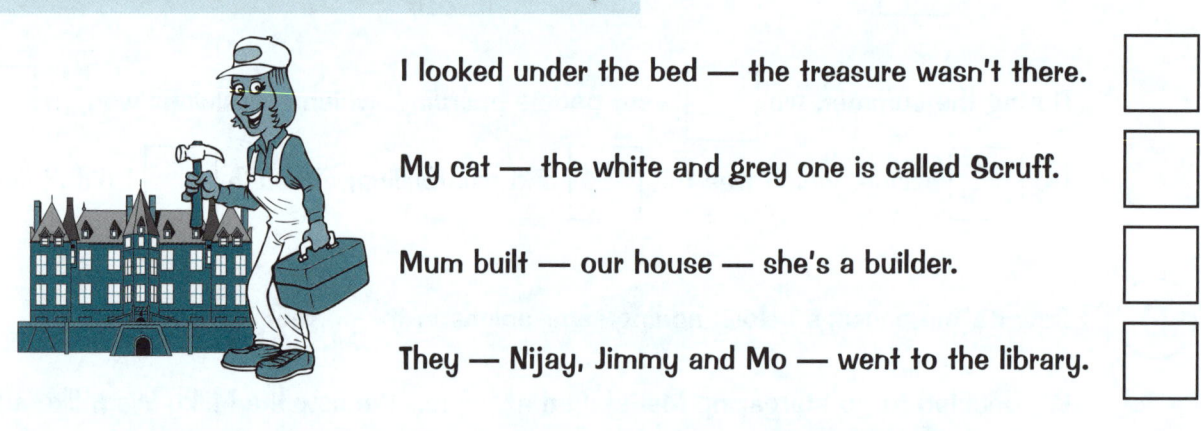

3 Tick the sentences that use dashes correctly.

I looked under the bed — the treasure wasn't there. ☐

My cat — the white and grey one is called Scruff. ☐

Mum built — our house — she's a builder. ☐

They — Nijay, Jimmy and Mo — went to the library. ☐

4 Each of these sentences needs a hyphen. Put one into the correct box.

I went to the ☐ book group to meet ☐ like ☐ minded people.

Kelsey gave her ☐ sister a hand ☐ made birthday ☐ present.

Frida Kahlo is my ☐ favourite twentieth ☐ century ☐ artist.

The robber left ☐ empty ☐ handed after being chased ☐ by the owner's ferret.

Section Two — Punctuation

Punctuation Practice

5 Put a cross next to the sentences that <u>do not</u> use apostrophes <u>correctly</u>. Write out the incorrect words correctly on the line.

Its not my fault that the crocodile escaped. ☐ ....

The three boy's sleeping bags lay on the floor. ☐ ....

"It's a good idea to trim its claws," said the vet. ☐ ....

Mustafa is ill so well stay at home. ☐ ....

You should've cut Callums' hair shorter. ☐ ....

6 Complete each sentence with either a colon or a semi-colon.

Genevieve made brownies ...... Huw ate them.

That tree is going to fall down ...... the trunk is rotten.

Sasha wants to go next door ...... they've got a new puppy.

Abasi plays the cello well ...... I don't.

Henry had three homes ...... London, Milan and Slough.

7 Punctuate this passage with inverted commas, full stops and commas.

I'm bored said Cat as she slowly leant back on the sofa

Let's go and explore in the garden suggested Sanav

Okay replied Cat It's got to be better than sitting around here

As they went outside the sun came out and a rainbow lit the sky

Look at that rainbow said Sanav I bet there's a pot of gold at the end of this

I'll race you said Cat as she ran off

 Carry on the story from question 7. Include some speech between Cat and Sanav, and make sure you punctuate your writing correctly.

Section Two — Punctuation

Prefixes

Warm Up Questions

1) True or false? The spelling of a root word changes when you add a prefix. ....

2) What does the prefix bi- mean? ....

3) Draw lines from the prefixes to the correct roots.

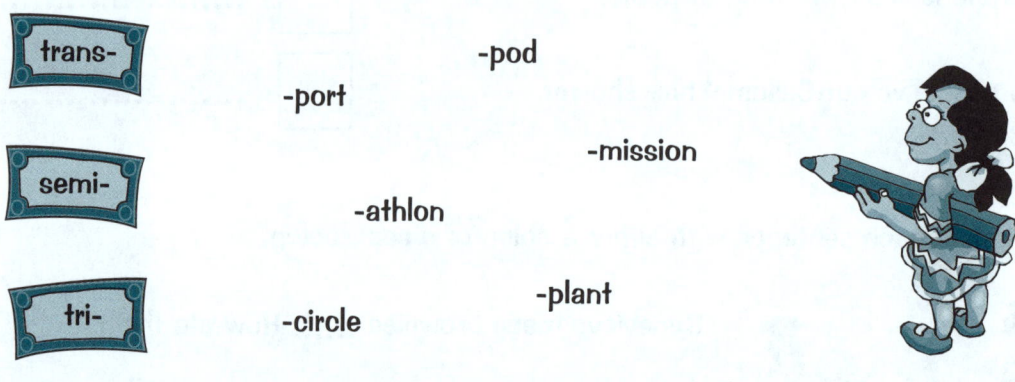

trans-   -pod
            -port
semi-   -mission
            -athlon
tri-   -plant
            -circle

Write the completed words on the dotted lines below.

....

....

4) Circle the correct word to complete the sentences below.

The council <u>transformed</u> / <u>triformed</u> the field into a new park.

Rohan wants a new <u>semicycle</u> / <u>bicycle</u> for his birthday.

The school hockey team reached the <u>trifinal</u> / <u>semifinal</u> of the tournament.

Lisa speaks three languages. She's <u>trilingual</u> / <u>bilingual</u> .

5) Complete the words in these sentences using trans-, bi- or tri-.

He cuts the cake into ....angular slices.

Band practice is ....weekly — it happens on Tuesdays and Thursdays.

The water was ....parent — you could see to the bottom of the lake.

Prefixes

6 Give the meaning of the prefix auto- in the words 'autograph', 'autobiography' and 'automated'.

....

7 Tick the boxes next to the sentences where every word is spelt correctly.

Jasmine wanted to be a micrographer when she was older. ☐

The team circumnavigated the globe in a tiny boat. ☐

I'd love to be able to aeroport to different places. ☐

The photocopier in the staff room has broken. ☐

8 Complete the words in these sentences using aero-, micro- or tele-.

Salim took the rabbit to the vet to see if it had a ....chip.

The rocket needs to be ....dynamic so that it will fly well.

The ....phone rang loudly in the silent house.

9 Add a hyphen to the words in the box below, then use them to complete the sentences.

> cooperate   reevaluate   deice

My mum had to .... the car before we could leave.

Tony was starting to .... his decision to join the circus.

The pirate decided she had to .... with her enemies.

Now Try This Hyphens can show that two similar words have different meanings, e.g. react and re-act. Use a dictionary to find as many words like this as you can in five minutes.

Section Three — Spelling

Words ending in 'shus' and 'shul'

Warm Up Question

1 Underline the word that is spelt incorrectly below.

precious　　　　essential　　　　residencial　　　　ambitious

2 Circle the words below that are spelt correctly.

suspicious　　　　anctious　　　　malixious　　　　cautious

infectious　　　　nutricious　　　　gracious　　　　vivatious

3 Complete the words in these sentences using -cious, -tious or -xious.

Tigers are very fero.......... animals.

Dani was usually shy, but she never felt self-cons.......... on stage.

Andy is very conscien.......... about his work.

Gertrude was a very obno.......... person.

4 Fill in the missing letter to finish each word correctly.

spe....ial　　　　ini....ial　　　　finan....ial　　　　gla....ial

confiden....ial　　　　par....ial　　　　so....ial　　　　poten....ial

5 Circle the correct spelling of each word to complete the sentences below.

The official / offitial spokesperson denied the alien sighting.

This drink contains no artifitial / artificial flavourings.

My favourite film was a big commercial / commertial success.

Meera is an influential / influencial member of our class.

The latest games console costs a substancial / substantial amount of money.

Words ending in -ant and -ent

1) Tick the boxes next to the words that are spelt correctly.

connfident ☐   assistant ☐   observent ☐

tolerant ☐   pregnent ☐   argument ☐

2) Circle the correct spelling of each word to complete the sentences below.

The museum was full of <u>anciant</u> / <u>ancient</u> dinosaur fossils.

Alfie put on <u>deodorant</u> / <u>deodorent</u> before he went out.

3) Sort the letters below into the right order to spell words ending in -ant or -ent.

(letters: t, s, n, i, d, a, t) ....

(letters: t, c, c, d, i, n, a, e) ....

4) Add either -ant or -ent to each of these words, then write the word in a sentence.

perman..........

....

eleph..........

....

independ..........

....

Now Try This: Think of a sentence that uses two words with the ending -ant and a sentence that uses two words with the ending -ent. Try to use words that aren't on this page.

Section Three — Spelling

-ance, -ancy, -ence and -ency

Warm Up Question

1 Underline the word below that is spelt correctly.

tolerence   intelligance   arrogance   distence

2 Complete the words in these sentences using -ance, -ancy, -ence or -ency.

The strict teacher demanded obedi.......... from all his pupils.

I'm not convinced about my sister's innoc.......... — I think she ate the cake.

There was a sense of urg.......... about the search for the missing kangaroo.

The decision to knock down the house was met with resist.......... .

Can you please explain your abs.......... from school last week?

3 Use the pictures to work out each word ending in -ance, -ancy, -ence or -ency. Complete the words on the dotted lines.

 sci............    inf............    bal............

4 Some of the words in this passage are spelt incorrectly. Circle the incorrect words and write the correct versions on the line below.

My cousin saw a vacency for a part-time job in the newspaper. It was a position in a chocolate factory. At the interview, she had to provide evidence that she liked chocolate, which she said was a nuisence. I told her that I would have done it for her! The job is quite boring at the moment — she just checks that the chocolates have the right consistancy — but it should get better in the future.

....

Section Three — Spelling

-able, -ible, -ably and -ibly

1 Use the suffixes in the shells to complete the words.

-able   -ible

comfort..........   respons..........   ed..........   miser..........

2 Tick the boxes next to the words that are spelt correctly.

considerably ☐   visibly ☐   impossably ☐

suitibly ☐   horrably ☐   audibly ☐

3 Circle the correct spelling of each word to complete the sentences below.

Our dog has a very recognisible / recognisable tail.

The football supporters are remarkably / remarkibly loud today.

Jenny has a hat that will turn you invisible / invisable !

We had to dress sensably / sensibly for the hike.

You sent me a letter, but your writing wasn't legible / legable .

4 Fill in the gaps in the sentences below using the correct words from the box.

> fashionable / fashionible   irresistable / irresistible
> terrably / terribly   capably / capibly

The game of hide-and-seek went .... — I got stuck in the shed.

Chidozie always wore very .... clothes.

My uncle baked a cake for my birthday. It was ....

Tammi handled the problem very ....

Now Try This — How many more words can you think of that end in -able, -ible, -ably or -ibly? Make a list on a separate piece of paper.

Adding Suffixes to Words Ending in -fer

Warm Up Questions

1) What is the suffix in the word 'preference'? ....

2) Give two more suffixes that you can add to words ending in -fer.

   ....

3) Add the suffixes to the world below and then write the words out in full.

   You may need to change the spelling of the root word.

   refer ➕ -ed / -ing / -al → ....

   ....

   ....

4) Underline the words below that are spelt <u>incorrectly</u>. Then write the <u>correct</u> spellings on the dotted lines.

   bufferring   referrence
           prefered   sufferring
                   offered
   transferring   inference
                   differred

   ....
   ....
   ....
   ....
   ....

5) Sort the letters below into the right order to spell words ending with -fer.

   (d, f, r, e, e) ....

   (f, c, o, r, n, e) ....

'ei' and 'ie' Words

1 Complete the words below using either 'ei' or 'ie'.

t......r   forf......t   y......ld   th......f

rel......f   h......st   n......ther   l......sure

2 Use the pictures to work out each word containing 'ei' or 'ie'.

w......ght   r......ndeer   sh......ld

3 Tick the boxes next to the words that are spelt correctly.

seize ☐   glaceir ☐   science ☐

hygeine ☐   weird ☐   protien ☐

4 One word has been misspelt in each of the sentences below.
Rewrite the sentences on the dotted lines so that all of the words are spelt correctly.

I can't believe my sunflower has reached a hieght of 200 cm.

....

We stopped breifly on our way through the fields.

....

They offer a vareity of soups with either bread or crisps.

....

Now Try This Not including the words on this page, create a list of as many words that contain 'ei' or 'ie' as you can think of in two minutes.

Words with 'ough' in

Warm Up Question

1 Circle the sound that the 'ough' makes in the word 'trough'.

'uff'   'ow'   'off'   'or'   'oh'

2 Draw lines to match each word to the 'ough' sound it makes.

fought   thoughtful

'or'

enough   nought

tough   bought

'uff'

ought   roughly

3 Sort the letters below into the right order to spell words which contain 'ough'.

 ....    ....

4 Complete the sentences below by filling in the missing 'ough' words.

borough   plough   brought   drought   throughout

She went to riding classes .... the summer.

Jonah bought a new .... for the farm.

Helena .... a present and some balloons to the party.

After the .... , the villagers were glad to see rain.

Next year, we're moving to a different .... of Greater Manchester.

Section Three — Spelling

Words with Silent Letters

1) Circle the correct spelling of each word to complete the sentences below.

One of my dads is a secretary and the other is a billder / builder .

Lisa has drawn a new desine / design for her rocket.

The national flower of Scotland is a thistle / thissle .

2) Tick the boxes next to the words that are spelt correctly.

knight ☐	garantee ☐	thum ☐
narly ☐	autumn ☐	written ☐
asend ☐	ourly ☐	could ☐

Write the correct spellings of the words that are spelt incorrectly in the box below.

3) Complete the words in these sentences by adding the missing silent letters.

Samia beat a steady r.....ythm on the drums.

The best biscuits were all hidden in the back of the cu.....board.

The g.....ard chased the thief through the museum.

Bao got a .....nitted jumper from his grandparents every birthday.

Now Try This — Make a list of as many other words as you can think of that contain silent letters.

Section Three — Spelling

Confusing Nouns and Verbs

Warm Up Question

1 What are nouns? Circle the correct answer below.

doing words   naming words

2 Sort the words below into nouns and verbs.

devise   license

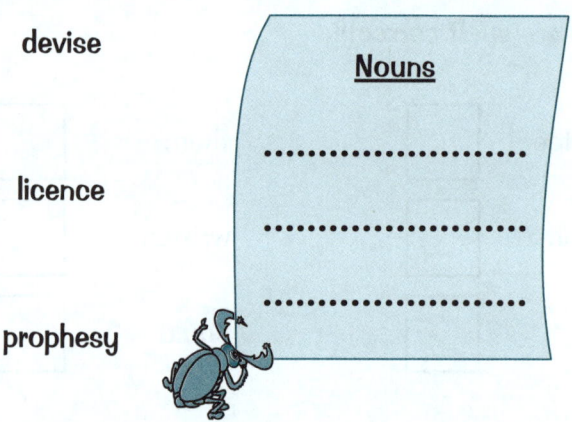
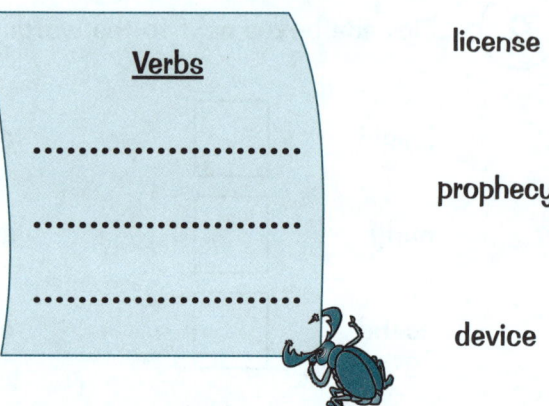

Nouns   **Verbs**

licence   prophecy

....

....

....

prophesy   device

3 Fill in the gaps in the sentences below using the correct words from the box.

practice   advice   advise   practise

Can I ask you for some .... about this problem?

Harvinder tries to .... his magic tricks every day.

They will .... you to eat more fruit and vegetables.

Kylie has had a lot of .... flying kites.

4 Complete the words in these sentences using 'ce' or 'se'.

The band practi..... their new songs every day after school.

My neighbour has invented an amazing devi..... that toasts bread in five seconds.

The council will licen..... you to organise a street party this summer.

Don't forget that we have hockey practi..... after school today.

Joanna is very forgetful — she didn't bring her driving licen..... or her passport.

Section Three — Spelling

Homophones

1 Fill in the gaps in the sentences below using the correct words from the box. Use each word once.

> waste   waist   grown   groan   bridle   bridal

The giraffe was so tiny that it only came up to her ....

My sister stayed in the .... suite before her wedding.

Ron thought the competition was a .... of time.

This pumpkin is the biggest one that I have ever ....

Ibrahim needed a new .... for his horse.

She let out a .... when she saw the score.

2 Circle the correct word to complete the sentences below.

A thick <u>mist</u> / <u>missed</u> descended on the village.

Abigail has always wanted to <u>write</u> / <u>right</u> a novel.

Why do you eat <u>serial</u> / <u>cereal</u> every morning for breakfast?

The <u>assent</u> / <u>ascent</u> to the top of the mountain was difficult.

My grandfather made a big <u>profit</u> / <u>prophet</u> selling ice creams.

3 These clues all describe one word from a pair of homophones. Write the words being described on the dotted lines.

To employ someone. ....

Further above something. ....

> higher   hire

To look for a short time. ....

The best or highest point. ....

> peek   peak

 Find a homophone for each of the words below:

draft   medal   principle   weather   sent   compliment

Section Three — Spelling

Spelling Practice

Warm Up Question

1 Underline the prefixes in the sentence below.

I watched television during the transatlantic flight.

2 Complete the words in these sentences using -able, -ible, -ably or -ibly.

My friend has an ador.......... hamster and two goldfish.

The traffic jam made us unbear.......... late for the concert.

Yoga is a type of exercise that helps you become more flex.......... .

3 Circle the misspelt words below.

friend   receive   weild   riegn

deisel   consceince   neighbour   neice

4 Complete the words in these sentences with the correct 'shus' or 'shul' ending.

The boxer won without knocking his opponent uncons.......... .

Jade loved all sports, but mar.......... arts were her favourite.

The laboratory was full of dangerous chemicals and no.......... fumes.

5 Add the missing silent letter to complete each word.

mus....le   w....ine   ha....ved   ....onesty   g....itar   dou....t

6 Use the picture to work out each 'ough' word.

c..............   th..............   ....

Section Three — Spelling

Spelling Practice

7 Fill in the gaps in the sentences below by using the correct words from the box.

> hindrance / hindrence   tendancy / tendency

I tried to help my dad clean, but he said I was being a ....

Jack has a .... to talk a lot when he feels nervous.

8 Draw lines to match each option to the correct word ending.

eleg-   innoc-

                        -ant

obedi-   hesit-

                        -ent

vac-   pres-

9 Circle the correct spelling of each word to complete the sentences below.

There was a rather unusual guessed / guest at the hotel this week.

We visited the countryside for some peace / piece and quiet.

Sonali wanted some assistants / assistance with choosing the right pet.

10 Each of the words below is spelt incorrectly. Write the correct spellings on the dotted lines.

preferrence ....   defered ....

confering ....   transferrable ....

11 Add the missing hyphen to this word, then use the word in a sentence.

coown ⟶ ....

....

Now Try This — Think of two words that start with each of the prefixes below:

micro-   aero-   semi-   circum-   tri-

Progress Test 1

1 Use the prefixes in the box below to complete the words.

> photo-   circum-   aero-   tele-

..........plane   ....vise   ....copy   ....stance

4 marks

2 Write a list of three things you could do next year using bullet points.

Next year I'm planning to: ....

....

....

3 marks

3 Circle the correct spelling of each word to complete the sentences below.

Kweku tripped over and injured his heal / heel last night.

That field used to be the sight / site of the old castle.

Is it possible to alter / altar the size of this shirt?

The special effects / affects in this TV series are amazing.

4 marks

4 Sort the letters below into the right order to spell a word ending in -cious or -tious.

(shield: p, r, o, u, s, e, i, c)   ....

(shield: t, i, a, o, u, b, m, s, i)   ....

2 marks

Progress Test 1

5 Circle the correct determiner to complete each sentence.

Out of the two scooters, he said that he prefers <u>this</u> / <u>those</u> one here.

Grace wants to buy <u>a</u> / <u>some</u> new jumper to replace her old one.

I looked everywhere for <u>that</u> / <u>a</u> shoe after you lost it yesterday.

3 marks

6 Tick the sentences that use dashes correctly.

Tibbles — my neighbour's cat always eats — our cat's food. ☐

We went to the shops — we needed more milk. ☐

The llama — who was called Sid — was very friendly. ☐

Gerald was sweeping the floor it — was dirty. ☐

2 marks

7 Complete each sentence with either a colon or a semi-colon.

I grow fruit in my garden .... apples, strawberries and oranges.

Tyson works as a florist .... Jenny is a firefighter.

Hockey practice was cancelled tonight .... it was raining too heavily.

3 marks

8 Tick the sentences that use the present perfect form.

Marie has driven two hundred miles to be here. ☐

They had never been on a boat. ☐

I have never seen that painting before. ☐

Ezra has written a poem. ☐

3 marks

Progress Test 1

9 Rewrite the sentence below, adding in apostrophes where they are needed.

I shouldnt have taken the dogs toy — that one is its favourite.

....

....

2 marks

10 Circle the correct words to complete each sentence in Standard English.

She wants to buy them / those ones over there.

Martin and I / me went to the woods to collect pine cones.

Aren't / ain't you supposed to be at drama club tonight?

They was / were winning the game of paintball.

This new robot toy was already broken / broke when I opened it.

5 marks

11 Complete the sentences below by adding main clauses. Remember to put commas in the correct places.

Every Wednesday ....

Shouting loudly ....

In the field ....

3 marks

12 Write a sentence about each picture using the past progressive.

....

....

....

2 marks

Progress Test 1

Progress Test 1

13 Choose the correct verb from the box below to complete the sentence in the subjunctive form.

> is   be   are

It is important that you .... quiet during the announcement.

1 mark

14 Punctuate these sentences with inverted commas, full stops and commas.

I think I'm going to go to the cinema tomorrow said Bilan

Val whispered Let's keep this a secret until the party

I saw two elephants said Alfie and a tiger as well

3 marks

15 Rewrite the sentences below in the passive voice.

Rosie bought a brand new motorbike.

....

We bought concert tickets.

....

2 marks

16 Some of the words in this passage are spelt <u>incorrectly</u>.
Circle the <u>incorrect</u> words and write the <u>correct</u> versions on the line below.

My best freind Aisha is very irresponsable. Last week, we went on a residencial trip to the Peak District with school. She got bored waiting for the safety demonstration to end and tried to clime a mountain by herself. If she'd been more patiant, she wouldn't have been in trouble!

....

....

5 marks

Score: ☐ /47

The Titanic

The *RMS Titanic* was a luxury passenger ship, built in Ireland, that set sail in 1912. On its first voyage, the ship struck an iceberg and sank, resulting in the deaths of hundreds of its passengers. This tragedy remains one of the world's most famous ocean disasters.

On 10th April, 1912, the *RMS Titanic* embarked from Southampton, England, bound for New York in the United States. For many, this momentous occasion was a cause for celebration.

5   The *Titanic*, operated by the White Star Line shipping company, was thought to be the grandest ship in existence, spanning an impressive 269 metres long (equivalent to the length of three football pitches) and containing state-of-the-art facilities for some of its wealthier passengers. It was also claimed that it would be nearly impossible for the *Titanic* to sink, which gave people the

10   impression that the ship was safe. However, this feeling of security was merely an illusion.

As the *Titanic* progressed on its voyage across the Atlantic Ocean, the crew received messages from other ships warning of icebergs in the vicinity. However, given the belief that the *Titanic* couldn't sink, the ship carried on at top speed, a mistake that would prove fatal. On the night of the 14th April, as the *Titanic* navigated its way through inky black waters, lookouts spotted

15   the dim shape of an iceberg directly in front of the ship. The crew desperately attempted to steer around the looming mountain of ice, but the ship's colossal weight and swift speed prevented it from moving in time, and the *Titanic* collided with the iceberg.

From that moment on, the *Titanic*'s demise was inevitable. The iceberg ripped a large hole in the side of the ship, and its compartments rapidly began filling with water. The crew was

20   now faced with another problem — the ship only had enough lifeboats for around half of its passengers, and the closest ship that was responding to the *Titanic*'s distress signals was hours away. As a result, hundreds of people were trapped on the sinking ship and, once the ship had sunk beneath the surface, stranded in the icy ocean. Due to the water's low temperature, most of these people perished.

25   In total, around 700 of the approximately 2200 people on board survived the sinking of the *Titanic*, with over 1500 losing their lives. In the aftermath of the tragedy, laws were passed making it a legal requirement for ships to carry enough lifeboats to accommodate everyone on board, in the hopes of preventing a similar disaster from occurring in the future.

Written by Rebecca Greaves

The Titanic

Warm Up Question

1 In lines 1-5, which verb does the writer use that means 'set off'?

....

2 Write down one reason why people thought the *Titanic* was a great ship.

....

3 Find and copy an example of alliteration from lines 11-17.

....

4 Do you think the lookouts could see the iceberg easily? Explain your answer.

....

....

5 What impression does the word "looming" (line 16) give of the iceberg?

....

6 How do you think the people back in England felt when they found out that the *Titanic* had sunk? Explain your answer.

....

....

Now Try This Aside from having more lifeboats, give two other things that could have been changed to make the *Titanic* safer. Explain how each improvement would have increased safety.

Section Four — Comprehension

Letter by Serena Williams

Serena Williams is an American tennis player. She has won more Grand Slam titles than any other current player, and has also won multiple gold medals in the Olympic Games. In this letter, written in 2016, she discusses the obstacles that women still face in sport.

To all incredible women who strive for excellence,

When I was growing up, I had a dream. I'm sure you did, too. My dream wasn't like that of an average kid, my dream was to be the best tennis player in the world. Not the best "female" tennis player in the world.

5   I was fortunate to have a family that supported my dream and encouraged me to follow it. I learned not to be afraid. I learned how important it is to fight for a dream and, most importantly, to dream big. My fight began when I was three and I haven't taken a break since.

But as we know, too often women are not supported enough or are discouraged from choosing their path. I hope together we can change that. For me, it was a question of resilience. What
10 others marked as flaws or disadvantages about myself – my race, my gender – I embraced as fuel for my success. I never let anything or anyone define me or my potential*. I controlled my future.

So when the subject of equal pay comes up, it frustrates me because I know firsthand that I, like you, have done the same work and made the same sacrifices as our male counterparts. I would never want my daughter to be paid less than my son for the same work. Nor would you.

15 As we know, women have to break down many barriers on the road to success. One of those barriers is the way we are constantly reminded we are not men, as if it is a flaw. People call me one of the "world's greatest female athletes". Do they say LeBron* is one of the world's best male athletes? Is Tiger*? Federer*? Why not? They are certainly not female. We should never let this go unchallenged. We should always be judged by our achievements, not by our gender.

20 For everything I've achieved in my life, I am profoundly grateful to have experienced the highs and lows that come with success. It is my hope that my story, and yours, will inspire all young women out there to push for greatness and follow their dreams with steadfast resilience. We must continue to dream big, and in doing so, we empower the next generation of women to be just as bold in their pursuits.

25 *Serena Williams*

A letter by Serena Williams, from www.theguardian.com

Glossary

potential — ability to develop or succeed	LeBron — LeBron James, a basketball player
Tiger — Tiger Woods, a golfer	Federer — Roger Federer, a tennis player

Section Four — Comprehension

Letter by Serena Williams

Warm Up Question

1 Circle the word which could best replace "strive" (line 1).

suffer   judge   fight   study

2 What does Williams say that she was lucky to have as a child?

....

3 Suggest a noun that could be used instead of "resilience" (line 9).

....

4 Write down two things that Williams faced criticism for.

....

5 Which of the following adjectives best describes Williams? Circle one.

determined   idle   unsporting   selfish

6 Why does Williams believe that men and women in sport deserve equal pay? Explain your answer with evidence from the text.

....

....

7 In your own words, summarise the vision of the future Williams outlines in lines 20-24.

....

....

Now Try This What effect does Serena Williams's letter have on the reader? Explain your answer.

A Connecticut Yankee in King Arthur's Court

A Connecticut Yankee in King Arthur's Court is a novel by Mark Twain. It follows the adventures of Hank Morgan, a man from Hartford, Connecticut (USA), who time travels to King Arthur's England. In this extract, Hank has just woken up in his new surroundings.

When I came to again, I was sitting under an oak tree, on the grass, with a whole beautiful and broad country landscape all to myself — nearly. Not entirely; for there was a fellow on a horse, looking down at me — a fellow fresh out of a picture-book. He was in old-time iron armour from head to heel, with a helmet on his head the shape of a nail-keg* with slits in it; and he had a shield, and a sword, and a prodigious* spear; and his horse had armour on, too, and a steel horn projecting from his forehead, and gorgeous red and green silk trappings* that hung down all around him like a bedquilt, nearly to the ground.

"Fair sir, will ye joust*?" said this fellow.

"Will I what?"

"Will ye try a passage of arms for land or lady or for—"

"What are you giving me?" I said. "Get along back to your circus, or I'll report you."

Now what does this man do but fall back a couple of hundred yards and then come rushing at me as hard as he could tear, with his nail-keg bent down nearly to his horse's neck and his long spear pointed straight ahead. I saw he meant business, so I was up the tree when he arrived.

He allowed that I was his property, the captive of his spear. There was argument on his side — and the bulk of the advantage — so I judged it best to humour him. We fixed up an agreement whereby I was to go with him and he was not to hurt me. I came down, and we started away, I walking by the side of his horse. We marched comfortably along, through glades and over brooks which I could not remember to have seen before — which puzzled me and made me wonder — and yet we did not come to any circus or sign of a circus. So I gave up the idea of a circus, and concluded he was from an asylum*. But we never came to an asylum — so I was up a stump, as you may say. I asked him how far we were from Hartford. He said he had never heard of the place; which I took to be a lie, but allowed it to go at that. At the end of an hour we saw a far-away town sleeping in a valley by a winding river; and beyond it on a hill, a vast grey fortress, with towers and turrets, the first I had ever seen out of a picture.

"Bridgeport?" said I, pointing.

"Camelot," said he.

An adapted extract from *A Connecticut Yankee in King Arthur's Court*, by Mark Twain

Glossary

nail-keg — a barrel for nails

trappings — decorations and ornaments

asylum — in the past, a hospital for people with mental illnesses

prodigious — extremely big

joust — a fight on horseback

A Connecticut Yankee in King Arthur's Court

Warm Up Question

1 In the first paragraph, which verb does the writer use that means "sticking out"?

....

2 Find and copy an example of a simile from lines 3-7.

....

....

3 "a far-away town sleeping in a valley" (line 25) is an example of (circle one):

a metaphor   alliteration   a simile   personification

4 Put these events in order (1-3) as they happen in the text.

Hank is taken prisoner by the knight. ☐

Hank wakes up in an unfamiliar place. ☐

Hank climbs up a tree. ☐

5 What do you think will happen next in the story? Explain your answer.

....

....

....

 How does the author make Camelot seem interesting? Explain your answer.

Section Four — Comprehension

Poems about the Battle of Britain

These poems are about the Battle of Britain, which was fought between British and German planes during the Second World War. Many of the air battles, known as 'dogfights', took place near or over the English Channel, where both poems are set.

The Battle of Britain

At sunrise, the pilot embarked,
Entranced by the air raid sirens.
"For king and country," the young man remarked,
His heart roaring like a lion's.

5   The planes' engines sputtered to life,
Unaware of the glory to gain.
Ready for the early, dawn-lit flight —
Spitfire, Defiant, Hurricane*.

He was told to defend the English Channel,
10 But what he'd face was a mystery.
Fingers flitting over control panels:
Final checks, then a flight into history.

Frantic — there was no time to wait,
He thrust and the craft surged forward.
15 A marshal* waved a flag in a figure of eight,
Directing the fighter planes shoreward.

Lift-off. Trees. Roads. Fields.
For his country he would pass over,
The world zipping by in the blink of an eye,
20 And the sun-drenched White Cliffs of Dover.

Glossary
Spitfire, Defiant, Hurricane — types of planes
marshal — someone who directs planes
buoyed — kept afloat

On Dover Beach

The boys rushed to the shore ecstatically,
Each bearing a pocketful of stones.
They marched with sights set on the sea,
Their laden shorts rattling like bones.

5   They looked out towards the rising sun
And watched each stone dance on the waves.
The rocks seemed to slip from their earthly bonds
Before sinking to watery graves.

Suddenly, engines pierced the silence
10 From behind the towering cliffs of white.
A flock of steel swallows; hulking metal giants
Soared in neat formation to the light.

How quickly those beasts seemed to fade away,
The roar of engines soon became a sigh.
15 Buoyed* only for a time that fateful day,
Like silver stones skipping on a sea of sky.

Written by James Summersgill

Section Four — Comprehension

Poems about the Battle of Britain

Warm Up Question

1) At what time of day are both poems set?

   ....

2) What does the word "entranced" (line 2) suggest about the pilot in *The Battle of Britain*?

   ....

   ....

3) Why do you think the poet uses lots of short sentences in line 17 of *The Battle of Britain*?

   ....

4) Which poem seems more exciting? Explain your answer.

   ....

   ....

5) Why do you think the verb "pierced" is used to describe the engines in *On Dover Beach*?

   ....

6) Why do you think that the poet compares the planes to skipping stones in lines 13-16 of *On Dover Beach*?

   ....

   ....

Now Try This — Which of the two poems do you think has the best description? Explain your answer.

The Shapeshifter: Running the Risk

> *The Shapeshifter: Running the Risk* is a novel by Ali Sparkes. It focuses on a group of children who have extraordinary abilities, including Dax, who can shapeshift into a fox. In this extract, Dax is in his fox form and is being chased by a pack of hunting hounds.

Dax fled down a steep embankment of ash and elder, his paws barely making contact with the earth, he moved so fast. He remembered that hounds found it hard to follow a scent through water, and he could smell a stream not far away, coursing through the lowest part of this woodland. He ducked under some brambles, feeling the jagged
5   thorns catch at the points of his ears and sending several smaller creatures scattering in terror as a predator thundered through their world.

He had to flatten almost to his belly to clear the underside of the brambles, which knotted themselves along the woodland floor for several yards, but a glint of white and brown movement caught his eye as he scrambled out from under the thorns — the water!
10 Dax plunged into it, sending a small tidal wave across the shallow pebbly bed of the stream. Too noisy! He could *feel* the hounds respond and veer in his direction; he could smell the excitement in them. Dax turned west and ran along the stream, one second up to his ankles, and the next almost to his haunches and swimming when the silt and pebbles sank suddenly downwards. The swimming was agonizingly slow.

15 *Shift! Shift!* urged a voice inside his head, which he recognized as Owen's. It made perfect sense, but Dax was terrified of stopping, and although he tried to push the shift, it wouldn't come. He needed to stop — breathe evenly — make it so — and he wasn't sure that he had time. He could clearly hear the dogs crashing through the brambles now, and the excited shouts of the hunt not far behind them. The fear that
20 pulsed through him was unlike anything he'd ever experienced. It made his insides feel like water and his head cloud with confusion. One strand of his strength seemed to buckle and fall away from him, giving in. If another strand — and then another — followed, he realized he would sink into the stream and prepare to die.

This awful weakness might have been his end, if he hadn't spotted a hole in the
25 bank. It was a foxhole, no doubt about it. A tight one, which maybe the hounds could not get through; he didn't know. The vixen had not gone into it; there was no recent scent. Dax didn't pause. He hurled himself from the water, straight into the hole. The smooth darkness of the earth wrapped around him and he scrambled deep, deep, and deeper into it. Small roots brushed his snout and ears and gave him a clawhold, as he
30 pushed further into the ground. Gone to ground. That was what they called it. Dax's fear chased him, snapping at his tail, but the earth, its feel, its smell, and the dull echo of it in his ears, called to him, held him, was more comforting than any bed.

An extract from *The Shapeshifter: Running the Risk* by Ali Sparkes.

The Shapeshifter: Running the Risk

Warm Up Question

1) Which word best describes the mood of the extract? Circle one.

mysterious   frantic   joyous   glum

2) At the start of the extract, why does Dax want to find water?

....

3) Suggest a verb that could be used instead of "thundered" in line 6.

....

4) Read lines 15-17. How can you tell Owen and Dax are friends? Explain your answer.

....

5) Why do you think the author uses dashes in lines 15-23?

....

....

6) How does the foxhole make Dax feel? Explain your answer.

....

....

Now Try This: The title of Sparkes's book is *The Shapeshifter: Running the Risk*. Do you think this title is a good fit for the extract? Explain your answer using evidence from the text.

Section Four — Comprehension

The Pool

The Pool is a poem by British poet Andrew Fusek Peters. In this nature-focused poem, the narrator describes an outdoor adventure with their companions on a summer's day.

We wade through corn like tigers on fire,
And run the obstacle course of barbed wire,
To follow the stream in a winding dream,
Until in a corner, scooped like ice cream,
5   Under the alders*, a hidden pool,
I trail my fingers in the willowy cool.
The grass is bullied and nettles beaten,
Blankets laid for food to be eaten,
We leap like salmon* one, two, three,
10 Divebombers of this inland sea,
Hit the water, bodies froze,
Suddenly trout* are tickling toes,
The oak is a mast in the ship of shade,
Cows drift through the glassy* glade*,
15 Heads bent like old men reading the news,
As beyond, the hills hold distant views
Under the beaming fat lady sun,
Witch of warmth, conjuring fun,
Until she grows tired and a little bit low,
20 And daylight packs up, ready to go!
Oh why can't summer last forever,
And why can't we take home this river?
In twilight we stumble through itchy corn,
Get caught on barbed wire with trousers torn,
25 Sleepily falling into cars
To carry us home under rippling stars.

Andrew Fusek Peters

Glossary
alders — a type of tree
salmon — a type of fish
trout — a type of fish
glassy glade — a clear and open space

The Pool

Warm Up Question

1. Which option best describes the poem's rhyme scheme? Circle one.

   every two lines rhyme   all of the lines rhyme   no lines rhyme

2. Find and copy two examples of metaphor in the poem.

   ....

   ....

3. What does the verb "conjuring" (line 18) suggest about the sun?

   ....

4. In your own words, summarise what the narrator does on their day out.

   ....

   ....

   ....

5. Compare lines 9-12 and lines 23-26. What two moods are created in these lines?

   ....

   Choose one of the groups of lines above and explain how its mood is created.

   ....

   ....

 Does this poem make you want to go on a similar day out? Explain your answer.

Mary Shelley's Diary

Mary Shelley was the author of *Frankenstein*. In 1816, she visited Switzerland with her partner, Percy Shelley. They stayed in a house called Maison Chapuis, near the poet Lord Byron's residence, Villa Diodati. In her diary, Mary describes exploring the area.

Wednesday, July 24. — To-day is rainy; therefore we cannot go to Col de Balme*. About 10 the weather appears clearing up. Shelley and I begin our journey to Montanvert*. Nothing can be more desolate than the ascent of this mountain; the trees in many places having been torn away by avalanches, and some half leaning over others, intermingled with stones, present the appearance of vast and dreadful
5 desolation. It began to rain almost as soon as we left our inn. When we had mounted considerably we turned to look on the scene. A dense white mist covered the vale, and tops of scattered pines peeping above were the only objects that presented themselves. The rain continued in torrents. We were wetted to the skin; so that, when we had ascended halfway, we resolved to turn back. As we descended, Shelley went before, and, tripping up, fell upon his knee. This added to the weakness occasioned by a blow on
10 his ascent; he fainted, and was for some minutes incapacitated from continuing his route.

We arrived wet to the skin. I read *Nouvelles Nouvelles**, and write my story. Shelley writes part of letter.

* * *

Saturday, July 27. — It is a most beautiful day, without a cloud. We set off at 12. The day is hot, yet there is a fine breeze. We pass by the Great Waterfall, which presents an aspect of singular beauty.
15 The wind carries it away from the rock, and on towards the north, and the fine spray into which it is entirely dissolved passes before the mountain like a mist.

The other cascade has very little water, and is consequently not so beautiful as before. The evening of the day is calm and beautiful. Evening is the only time I enjoy travelling. The horses went fast, and the plain opened before us. We saw Jura* and the Lake*
20 like old friends. I longed to see my pretty babe. At 9, after much inquiring and stupidity, we find the road, and alight at Diodati. We converse with Lord Byron till 12, and then go down to Chapuis, kiss our babe, and go to bed.

An extract from Mary Shelley's diary

Glossary

Col de Balme — a mountain pass in the Alps
Nouvelles Nouvelles — a collection of French stories
the Lake — Lake Geneva, a lake in the Swiss Alps
Montanvert — a glacier
Jura — Swiss mountains

Mary Shelley's Diary

Warm Up Question

1 Why can't the Shelleys go to Col de Balme on July 24th? Circle one.

it is too hot   it is too wet   it is too cold

2 What do you think "desolate" (line 2) means? Check your answer in a dictionary.

....

3 What effect does Mary's description of the mountain in lines 2-5 have on the reader?

....

....

4 Suggest a verb that could be used instead of "ascended" in line 8.

....

5 Why do you think Mary only enjoys travelling in the evening? Explain your answer.

....

....

6 Find and copy an example of a simile from lines 17-22.

....

7 How do you think Mary felt when she returned to Maison Chapuis? Explain your answer.

....

....

Does this extract make you want to visit Switzerland? Explain your answer.

Interview with Quentin Blake

> Quentin Blake is an illustrator whose work has appeared in hundreds of children's books. He has illustrated books for many authors, including Michael Rosen, David Walliams and Roald Dahl. This is an extract from an interview given by Blake in 2020.

What advice would you give to aspiring illustrators?

Everybody can draw something. Some people are embarrassed because they think they're not very skilful, but what I say to them is: 'Draw what you can see in front of you'. If you look at it later, you'll be surprised at what you brought away from that person, that situation, that landscape. You've grasped something. It may not be what you thought you'd get to begin with, but that degree of concentration is very good for the system. I've been doing it for 75 years and it's continuously interesting.

How do you dream up ideas for new characters?

Introduce yourself to your characters by drawing them. If you're creating the character yourself, keep thinking about that character and the situation you've invented. The illustration will start to take on the character and you sort of meet them by drawing them. By the time you've finished the book it becomes somebody you know.

What's it like to work with an author and interpret* someone else's text?

A good illustration is one that both complements* and contrasts with the text. You need to form a double act with the author. The author is the main character though; as an illustrator, you have to play up to them. I had to do a lot of that with Roald Dahl's books. There's a point in *Matilda* where Trunchbull is so cross that she picks up a plate and smashes it over Bruce Bogtrotter's head. I chose to draw the moment when she lifted up the plate, not the bit where she hits him with it, because that's the writer's moment. Your job is to work around that.

I didn't know Roald Dahl very well for the first book or two. Somebody said he was a formidable* personality but this wasn't really a problem. I started visiting him at his home in Great Missenden and I'd do rough drawings of what I thought the characters would look like. We established a very good collaboration: we talked about the drawings and I was ready to change things. I'm not fussy like that — it's part of the job, after all — but we wanted the drawings to do part of the work. We were very different, but a lot of the humour was the same.

Are book covers important?

Don't judge a book by its cover... but do always appreciate its significance. This is an important aspect of good illustration and very interesting to me because drawing book covers is one of the most difficult things. You need to make the book look interesting and give a feeling of its atmosphere and flavour, but at the same time you don't want to say too much.

An extract from an interview with Quentin Blake, from www.bl.uk

---

Glossary

interpret — to work out the meaning of   complements — improves   formidable — scary

Interview with Quentin Blake

Warm Up Question

1) According to Blake, why are some people are embarrassed to draw? Circle one answer.

They've never done it before.   They're very shy.   They think they're bad at it.

2) What does Blake mean by "You've grasped something" (line 5)?

....

3) According to Blake, drawing characters (circle one):

is really difficult.   brings them to life.   makes them less realistic.

4) Do you think Blake enjoyed working with Roald Dahl? Explain your answer using evidence from the text.

....

....

....

5) In your own words, summarise what Blake says about book covers in lines 26-30.

....

....

6) In your own words, explain what you think Blake means by a book's "flavour" (line 30).

....

....

Now Try This What impression do you get of Blake from this interview? Explain your answer.

Section Four — Comprehension

Who Needs Luck?

This extract is from a play about a kind-hearted and nervous man called Fred Foglio, who has been cursed with a lifetime of bad luck. In this scene, Fred is attending an interview for a cleaning job at the zoo, but he soon finds himself involved in a bit of a mix-up.

Okeke: Stanley Moore, please come through.

Fred looks around him and sees that no one else is in the dingy office.

Fred: Me? I – I'm – My name is Fred. Yes, Frederick Foglio, I'm quite sure of it, Miss…?

Okeke: Miss Okeke. And you're Stanley. Look, it says it right there on your nametag.
5 Now, hurry yourself along; Mr Sunday doesn't like to be kept waiting.

Bewildered, Fred heads into the office as he studies the scrawled letters spelling out 'STANLEY' on the sticker adorning his sweatshirt.

Sunday: Stanley! What a delight it is to have you here — sit down.

Fred: Thank you, Mr… Sunday.

10 *Fred awkwardly pulls out a flimsy metal chair and sits.*

My name is actually Fred, though, Mr Sunday.

There is a long pause as Sunday studies Fred's incorrect nametag. Then his expression sours and he furrows his brow. Suddenly, he erupts in laughter as Fred watches in disbelief.

Sunday: Ha! Very good, Stanley! Very good! For a second there, you almost had me.
15 Sonya over at Flotsam Zoo told me you'd be as sharp as a tack.

Sunday continues to chuckle, before producing a handkerchief to wipe his eyes.

Right, I won't mince my words here. I want… *you!*

Sunday leans over the desk and prods the word 'STANLEY' into Fred's chest, before collapsing back into his deep leather chair and flicking through a stack of paper.

20 Your track record is impeccable*. Twenty-five years experience as a zookeeper —

Fred: Twenty-five years experience? But I'm only 34, Mr Sunday!

Sunday: Don't, Stanley. Please. You'll only set me off again. And for heaven's sake, call me Robert… or Bob. Ideally, the latter. Anyway, tell me: why do you want to work here? 'Cause I'm as sure as a tiger has stripes that it isn't for the pay!

25 *Sunday takes a big gulp of water to congratulate himself on his joke but swallows funnily and violently coughs. Fred ducks to avoid a shower of droplets.*

Fred: It's not for the pay. You see. I'm not even here for the zookeeper jo–

Sunday: Fantastic! I knew you weren't just after some quick cash. Now, you can start immediately and we'll discuss trivialities* like your salary and safety training later.
30 For now, would you mind taking some food to the alligators? They were meant to have been fed hours ago.

Written by James Summersgill

Glossary

impeccable — perfect   trivialities — unimportant things

Who Needs Luck?

Warm Up Question

1) Give one feature of the text that tells you it is a playscript.

....

2) How does Fred react to Miss Okeke in line 3? How can you tell?

....

3) Find and copy a simile from lines 8-21 which shows that Mr Sunday thinks Fred is clever.

....

4) Do you think Mr Sunday is a friendly man? Give reasons for your answer.

....

....

5) Why does Mr Sunday become convinced that he wants to hire Fred in lines 24-30?

....

....

6) Do you think Mr Sunday cares about his employees? Explain your answer.

....

....

 Do you think Fred will try to feed the alligators? Explain your answer.

Yorimasa and the Monster

This text written by F. Hadland Davis is based on a Japanese myth. The myth describes how the brave knight Yorimasa slays a monster, after its screeching made the Emperor ill.

A long time ago, a certain Emperor became seriously ill. He was unable to sleep at night owing to a most horrible and unaccountable noise he heard proceeding from the roof of the palace. A number of his courtiers* decided to lie in wait for this strange nocturnal visitor. As soon as the sun set they
5   noticed that a dark cloud crept from the eastern horizon, and alighted* on the roof of the palace. Those who waited in the imperial bed-chamber heard extraordinary scratching sounds, as if what had at first appeared to be a cloud had suddenly changed into a beast with gigantic and powerful claws.

Night after night this terrible visitor came, and night after night the Emperor grew worse.
10 He at last became so ill that it was obvious to all those in attendance upon him that unless something could be done to destroy this monster the Emperor would certainly die.

At last it was decided that Yorimasa was the one knight in the kingdom valiant* enough to relieve his Majesty of these terrible hauntings. Yorimasa accordingly made elaborate preparations for the fray*. He took his best bow and steel-headed arrows, donned his armour,
15 over which he wore a hunting-dress, and a ceremonial cap instead of his usual helmet.

At sunset, he lay hidden outside the palace. While he waited, thunder crashed overhead, lightning blazed in the sky, and the wind shrieked like a pack of wild demons. But Yorimasa was a brave man, and the fury of the elements in no way daunted* him. When midnight came he saw a black cloud rush through the sky and rest upon the roof of the palace. At the north-east corner it stopped.
20 Once more the lightning flashed in the sky, and this time he saw the gleaming eyes of a large animal. Noting the exact position of this strange monster, he pulled at his bow till it became as round as the full moon. In another moment his steel-headed arrow hit its mark. There was an awful roar of anger, and then a heavy thud as the huge monster rolled from the palace roof to the ground.

Yorimasa and his retainer* ran forward and despatched* the fearful creature they saw before them.
25 This evil monster of the night was as large as a horse. It had the head of an ape, and the body and claws were like those of a tiger, with a serpent's tail, the wings of a bird, and the scales of a dragon.

From the very moment the creature died the Emperor's health rapidly improved, and Yorimasa was rewarded for his services by being presented with a sword called Shishi-wo, which means "the King of Lions."

An adapted extract from *Myths & Legends of Japan*, by Frederick Hadland Davis

Glossary

courtiers — royal assistants	alighted — landed	valiant — brave
fray — a fight	daunted — frightened	retainer — servant

Yorimasa and the Monster

Warm Up Question

1 What does the word "nocturnal" (line 4) tell you about the monster? Circle one.

It comes out in the day   It never sleeps   It comes out at night

2 Why was Yorimasa asked to slay the monster?

....

3 Write down the items of clothing that Yorimasa wore to fight the monster.

....

4 Read lines 16-20. How does the writer create a scary atmosphere? Give examples.

....
....
....

5 How can you tell that Yorimasa is skilled with a bow and arrow?

....

6 What effect does the description of the monster in lines 24-26 have on the reader?

....
....

 What do you think Yorimasa did next? Explain your answer.

Section Four — Comprehension

How to Cut a Pomegranate

Imtiaz Dharker is a British poet. She was born in Pakistan, grew up in Glasgow and now lives in Britain and India. She has written several collections of poetry. In this poem, the narrator recalls a conversation with their father about the beauty of the pomegranate fruit.

'Never,' said my father,
'Never cut a pomegranate
through the heart. It will weep blood.
Treat it delicately, with respect.

5   Just slit the upper skin across four quarters.
This is a magic fruit,
so when you split it open, be prepared
for the jewels of the world to tumble out,
more precious than garnets*,
10   more lustrous than rubies,
lit as if from inside.
Each jewel contains a living seed.
Separate one crystal.
Hold it up to catch the light.
15   Inside is a whole universe.
No common jewel can give you this.'

Afterwards, I tried to make necklaces
of pomegranate seeds.
The juice spurted out, bright crimson,
20   and stained my fingers, then my mouth.

I didn't mind. The juice tasted of gardens
I had never seen, voluptuous*
with myrtle*, lemon, jasmine*,
and alive with parrots' wings.

25   The pomegranate reminded me
that somewhere I had another home.

Imtiaz Dharker

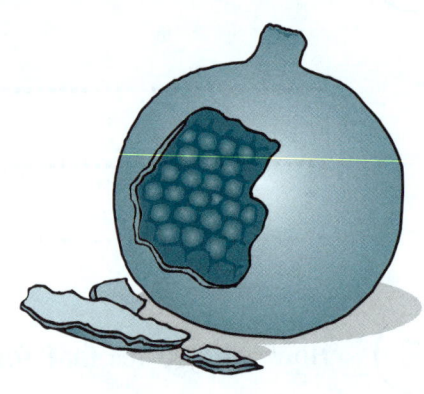

Glossary
garnet — a red gemstone
voluptuous — full
myrtle — a plant with white flowers and dark berries
jasmine — a plant with pale flowers

How to Cut a Pomegranate

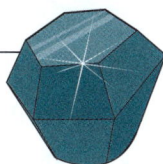

Warm Up Question

1 In which of these forms is the poem written? Circle one.

sonnet   free verse   rhyming couplets   haiku

2 Find and copy an example of personification from lines 1-5.

....

3 "the jewels of the world" (line 8) is an example of (circle one):

a simile   a metaphor   alliteration   onomatopoeia

4 What do you think "lustrous" (line 10) means? Check your answer in a dictionary.

....

5 Do you think that the narrator was a child or an adult when they had this conversation? Explain your answer.

....

....

6 How do you think the narrator's father felt about them spilling the juice in lines 17-20? Explain your answer.

....

....

Now Try This — Write a six-line stanza about your favourite fruit and how it makes you feel. Match the style and form of Dharker's poem in your stanza.

Section Four — Comprehension

A Daughter of the Samurai

A Daughter of the Samurai is a memoir by Etsu Inagaki Sugimoto. It recounts how nineteenth-century Japanese traditions influenced Sugimoto's upbringing. In this extract, Sugimoto describes the difficulties of helping her dog, Shiro, after he became ill.

I sat down on the edge of the porch and Shiro snuggled his cold nose into my long sleeve. We were two as disconsolate* creatures as could be found, and as I buried my hand in his rough white fur, I had to struggle hard to remember that a samurai's daughter does not cry.

Suddenly I recalled the saying, "To unreasonably relax is cowardice." I bounded up. I
5 talked to Shiro. I played with him. I even ran races with him in the garden. When at last I returned to the house I had reason to suspect that the family felt disapproval of my wild conduct, but because I was all dearness to my father I escaped reproof* for his sake. Everyone had a tender heart in those days; for the heaviness of dread was upon us all.

One day Shiro fell sick, and would eat nothing I put into his bowl. I had a childish feeling
10 that if he would eat he would get well, but that day happened to be the death anniversary of an ancestor, and was therefore a day of fasting. We had only vegetables for dinner, and so there were no good scraps for Shiro. As always when in trouble, I went to Ishi. She knew we ought not to handle fish on a fast day, but she pitied my anxiety and smuggled me some fish bones from somewhere. I took them to a distant part of the garden and crushed them between two flat stones.
15 Then I mixed them with bean soup from the kitchen and took them to the kindling shed where Shiro was lying on his straw mat. Poor Shiro looked grateful, but he would not get up; and thinking that perhaps he was cold, I ran to my room and brought my crepe* cushion to cover him.

When this became known to my grandmother, she sent for me to come to her room. The moment I lifted my face after bowing I knew this was not one of the times when I was to be
20 entertained with sweet bean-cake.

"Little Etsu-ko," she said (she always called me "Etsu-ko" when she spoke sternly), "I must speak to you of something very important. I am told that you wrapped Shiro with your silk cushion."

Startled at her tone, I meekly bowed.
25 "Do you not know," she went on, "that you are guilty of the utmost unkindness to Shiro when you do inappropriate things for him?"

I must have looked shocked and puzzled, for she spoke very gently after that, explaining that since white dogs belong to the order* next lower than that of human beings, my kindness might postpone for another lifetime* Shiro's being born in human shape.

An extract from *A Daughter of the Samurai* by Etsu Inagaki Sugimoto

Glossary

disconsolate — unhappy	the order — It was thought that certain types of living things were better than others.
reproof — criticism	
crepe — silk	another lifetime — Some people believe that living things can be reborn as something else after they die.

Section Four — Comprehension

A Daughter of the Samurai

Warm Up Question

1) How do you know that this text is a memoir? Circle one feature.

   dated entries   formal language   first-person narration   present tense

2) Why do you think the writer uses short sentences in lines 4-5?

   ....

   ....

3) In your own words, explain what you think "the heaviness of dread" (line 8) means.

   ....

4) How do you think the writer feels in lines 21-26? Give reasons for your answer.

   ....

   ....

5) What impression do you get of the writer's grandmother? Explain your answer.

   ....

6) Give one way that Ishi is different to the writer's grandmother.

   ....

   ....

 Would you like to be reborn as a different kind of animal?
Using the extract from Sugimoto's memoir to help you, explain your answer.

Section Four — Comprehension

Progress Test 2

Read the text, then answer the questions that follow.

Water Park Not So Watertight

Last night, residents of Rainham were astounded to learn that their homes sat atop the UK's most elaborate underground water park. The water park, of which the townspeople were unaware of until yesterday, was founded by Wade Brook, the leader of a secret society named the Water Babies.

5 When questioned about the society, Brook begrudgingly revealed that it is comprised of a select group of individuals, all of whom have three things in common — a hatred of public swimming pools, a desire to shoot down water-filled tunnels and, interestingly, a passion for interior design. Upon investigation, the water park has been found to be a space for artistic expression, as well as a feat of human engineering. The

10 majority of the tunnels have been studded with sparkling stones and illuminated by multicoloured lasers.

As to whether the venue was intended to be shared with the townspeople, Brook simply remarked, "No." The water park's existence was accidentally disclosed by one of the more talkative members of the Water Babies, who has since been exiled from the

15 group. Despite this mishap bringing misery to those who wanted to tunnel-surf in peace, news of the park's existence has been enthusiastically received by Rainham's residents.

"It sounds absolutely fantastic," Marina Fisher, a mother of three, told us. "Here in Rainham, outdoor activities are severely limited by the lack of sunshine. A water park would be a great rainy-day alternative that the whole family could enjoy."

20 Another resident, Jordan Poole, felt only relief. "For months, I've been wondering why I kept hearing the occasional 'whoop!' coming from the drains at the side of the road. Now I know I'm not going to be attacked by excitable gutter rats!" he exclaimed.

According to the mayor, preparations are currently being made for the water park to be opened up to the public. The Water Babies have also been put under surveillance,

25 as it is suspected that the group is planning another secret construction project.

Written by Rebecca Greaves

Progress Test 2

1 Suggest a phrase that could replace "a feat" (line 9).

....

1 mark

2 The phrase "studded with sparkling stones" (line 10) is an example of what technique?

....

1 mark

3 Give two features of the text that tell you it is a newspaper article.

....

2 marks

4 Find and copy a phrase from lines 12-16 which suggests that the Water Babies are unforgiving.

....

1 mark

5 In your own words, explain why Marina Fisher approves of the water park.

....

1 mark

6 Imagine you are a reporter. Would you rather interview Wade Brook or Jordan Poole? Explain your answer.

....

....

2 marks

7 What do you think the Water Babies will do next? Explain your answer.

....

....

2 marks

Progress Test 2

Progress Test 2

8 Write an antonym on the dotted line for each word below.

freezing → .... thoughtful → ....

confident → .... delicious → ....

interesting → .... orderly → ....

6 marks

9 Complete each sentence using the tense in brackets.

Shania .... her dogs around the park. (simple past tense)

Dominic .... pictures in art class. (simple present tense)

Ruth .... up the ladder. (present progressive tense)

3 marks

10 Rewrite the sentences below in the active voice.

The tennis ball was hit by Manali.

....

The llamas will be fed by us.

....

2 marks

11 Fill the gaps in this passage with the conjunctions in the box below. Only use each conjunction once.

> but   nor   because   and

Lucy entered the maze .... soon became lost. She tried going left .... the path looked promising, ... it only led to a dead end. Retracing her steps didn't help, ... did trying to peep over the hedges. Eventually, after much searching, she found the exit.

4 marks

Progress Test 2

Progress Test 2

12 Add commas in the correct places in the passage below.

Last week the king who is usually bad-tempered invited everyone to his palace for a celebration. Surprised by his change of heart I was suspicious and did not go.

4 marks

13 Each of these sentences needs a hyphen. Put one into the correct box.

I thought it would ☐ arrive ☐ early, but it was very last ☐ minute.

Her family ☐ owned business had ☐ existed for a ☐ century.

2 marks

14 Rewrite the sentences below, adding a semi-colon or a colon in the correct place.

They saw many sights a waterfall, a cave and a forest.

....

I chose to go kayaking Harriet went swimming.

....

2 marks

15 One word in each sentence is spelt wrong. Write the correct spellings on the lines.

It was crutial that the climbers reached the summit. ....

Gregorio never thought he would acheive so much. ....

Falling into mud is an unpleasent experience. ....

3 marks

16 Circle the correct word to complete the sentences so that they make sense.

They <u>sought</u> / <u>sort</u> the criminal.

That horse tends to <u>stair</u> / <u>stare</u> .

2 marks

Score: ☐ /38

Section Five — Drafting Your Work

Planning Your Writing

1 Draw lines to match each extract to the correct purpose.

The purpose of a text is the reason it's been written.

Purpose

- Persuade — If you're starting at university, you'll need to know how to cook. Otherwise, you may end up eating beans on toast every night.

- Entertain — Dad yawned loudly. Suddenly, the settee cushions clamped around him like a set of teeth. The settee was trying to eat Dad!

- Advise — Why use multiple utensils? Revolutionise how you eat with the all-new *Kniforkpoon*. A knife, a fork and a spoon all in one — buy yours now!

2 Draw lines to match each text to the most appropriate style of writing.

A letter from the mayor informing people about roadworks.   Descriptive language, building suspense.

A postcard to a family member telling them about a school trip.   Formal, serious language, lots of information.

A story about a pigeon who has to save the world.   Informal language, personal tone.

3 Number these parts of a report about cars to put them in a sensible order.

Earliest cars — slow, large, expensive and dangerous ☐

Introduction — what cars are, why people use them ☐

Conclusion — cars still very popular, more electric cars ☐

Cars improve — safety became a priority, more affordable ☐

Electric cars — recent invention, better for environment ☐

Now Try This — Plan a story about a cooking contest that will appeal to an audience of people your age.

Editing Your Work

Warm Up Question

1 Circle the things you should check while editing your work.

the text makes sense   sentences flow well together

every sentence is in the passive voice

2 This is the first draft of the start of a mystery story. Below are some suggestions of how it could be improved. Read the extract, and then read the suggestions.

Meera was a seven-year-old girl. She lived in a house with her mum, dad and older sister Alisha. One day, someone posted a strange package through her front door. Inside the package were a letter and a map. Meera read the letter. It contained a secret message.

- Change the first two sentences so that Meera is doing something interesting.
- Add some description about the setting, Meera, the letter and/or the person who posted the package.
- It would be more interesting to say what the letter said.
- Show how Meera felt after reading the letter.

Rewrite the extract, using the suggestions above to make it better.

....
....
....
....
....
....
....
....
....

Section Five — Drafting Your Work

Editing Your Work

3 This is an extract from a report about famous buildings. Label any changes that would make it better.

You could split up or combine sentences, group ideas into paragraphs, use pronouns to avoid repetition or use more interesting words.

The Leaning Tower of Pisa is in Italy. The tower is one of Italy's most popular tourist destinations. Architects began building the tower in the 12th century. They quickly noticed that the tower had started to lean. The ground underneath the tower was very soft. The tower began leaning more and more as time passed. In the 1990s, the tower was fixed and made stronger. Millions of people visit the tower and take pictures of themselves pretending to hold up the leaning tower.

Write a second draft of this extract based on the changes you've suggested.

....

....

....

....

....

....

....

....

....

....

Now Try This: Write a letter to your local council complaining about a flock of thieving magpies. Swap your letter with a friend and suggest changes to each other's work.

Section Five — Drafting Your Work

Proofreading Your Work

Warm Up Question

1 Underline the mistakes in these sentences.

"Bewear of theives and pirates once you reach the port?" the captain yelled.

2 This is a draft of an extract from a science fiction story. Circle each mistake and write the correction above it.

The spaceship cruised around the dusty, red planet for the third time that day. In the cockpit, several creatures were huddled around a tall woman waring a navy flight helmet.

Are you sure they landed on Mars, Commander." a wrinkly, blob-like creature at the back off the crowd tentative asked.

"Theyve got to be here!" the woman retorts through gritted teeth.

On another day, she might of made an example of the rude blob, but she had other things on her mind. She pulled up the visor on her helmet and began scanning the ground. A long, tence silence hung over the cockpit.

"There! That's there ship! Prepare for landing," the commander grinned, eager to finally catch the crooks who had stolen her laser goggles

A siren wailed as a banshee and the room was filled with a crimson red light. The creatures scrambled to acsion, pressing various switches and buttons before strapping themselfs into their seat's. a mighty rumble came from behind them as the endgines fired up. The spaceship suddenly begun accelerating to wards the planet, bearly allowing time for some creatures to put their seatbelts on.

Section Five — Drafting Your Work

Magical Mystery Tours

Warm Up Question

1 Circle the purpose of an advert.

To entertain customers   To persuade customers   To advise customers

2 This is an extract from an advert. Read the extract, then fill in the table below.

Can't think of the next place to visit? Tired of the same old boring holidays? Then you need Magical Mystery Tours! Let Magical Mystery Tours whisk you away to some spellbinding locations. Sun, sea and sand or mountains, moors and meadows; a faraway kingdom or an underwater exploration — Magical Mystery Tours will take you on a holiday you'll never forget!

Technique	Example from the extract	Effect of the technique
Repetition		
List of three		

3 These are more sentences from the advert. Rewrite each one using the technique in brackets to make it more persuasive.

You'll have an adventure. (Exaggeration)

....

You can choose your own route. (Rhetorical question)

....

Magical Mystery Tours

4 Read the rest of the advert below, then rewrite it to make it more persuasive.

Your job is boring so you want a holiday. Magical Mystery Tours will give you a break from the mundane. Magical Mystery Tours has something for everyone of any age. A fair price for a good holiday.

....
....
....
....
....

5 Magical Mystery Tours are bringing out a new product — Magical Sunglasses. Write an advert persuading people to buy this product. Use repetition, exaggeration, lists of three and rhetorical questions to make the advert as persuasive as possible.

....
....
....
....
....
....
....
....
....
....

Now Try This Write an advert for your favourite toy or game. Make it as persuasive as you can.

Section Six — Non-Fiction

The Beautiful Game

Warm Up Question

1 Circle the adverbial in the sentence below.

Lastly, I would like to show you the photos of my cats and dogs.

2 Circle the correct option to complete the adverbials and help the text flow.

The football World Cup is the biggest football tournament in the world / last year. National teams play qualifiers each year / country to determine which teams will feature in the tournament, usually / tomorrow in the autumn and spring. The World Cup is traditionally held in the summer / moon and lasts for five weeks / twice a week.

3 Read this extract from the same text. Underline the places where the text would flow better if repeated nouns were replaced with pronouns.

Just before the 1966 football World Cup was held in England, the Jules Rimet Trophy was stolen. The Jules Rimet Trophy was to be awarded to the World Cup winners. Pickles, a male collie cross, was walking with his owner one day when Pickles sniffed out the trophy! Pickles was already famous by the time that England won the World Cup that year and Pickles also went on to star in a film.

Rewrite the extract using pronouns.

....
....
....
....
....
....

The Beautiful Game

4 Complete the passage below using the linking words in the box.

> when   for example   although

The Euros is another tournament played every four years, ... only European countries take part. The Soviet Union won the first tournament in 1960, ... it was hosted by France. The host country changes every tournament, ... , it was first held in England in 1996.

5 Read the paragraph below and choose which of the three following sentences links best to the original paragraph. Put a tick next to the right one.

During World War One, women's football grew in popularity. One famous team was 'Dick, Kerr Ladies FC', who drew a crowd of 53 000 supporters on Boxing Day in 1920.

'Dick, Kerr Ladies FC' were really popular. ☐

'Dick, Kerr Ladies FC' are really popular. ☐

'Dick, Kerr Ladies FC' will be really popular. ☐

6 Write letters in the boxes to show which sentences belong in the same paragraphs.

a) Football teams often have local rivalries.
b) England's men are 'The Three Lions'.
c) One famous rivalry is between Liverpool and Everton.
d) National teams often have nicknames.
e) Derby matches are usually tense games.
f) And the women's team are 'The Lionesses'.
g) The Australian teams also have nicknames — the 'Socceroos' and the 'Matildas'.
h) A match between rival teams is a 'derby'.

Paragraph 1: | a | | | |

Paragraph 2: | d | | | |

Now Try This Think of a machine. Explain what it does and how to use it. Use pronouns, adverbials, linking words and phrases, and tense choices to make your text flow.

Section Six — Non-Fiction

Blue Whales

Warm Up Questions

1 Circle the sentence below that is a generalisation.

A generalisation is something that is true in most cases.

Hadrian's Wall is in the north of England.   Most children dislike Brussels sprouts.

2 True or false? Objective writing gives personal opinions rather than facts.

....

3 Read this extract from a report about blue whales. Fill in the gaps to turn these sentences into generalisations. Use the words and phrases in the box.

Blue whales can be found in .... of the world's oceans. Some people think that there will soon be so many ships in the ocean that blue whales will .... find getting around difficult. Blue whales are .... solitary creatures but they .... found in pairs as well.

> can be
> sometimes
> nearly all
> typically

4 Here is another extract from the report. Underline all the opinions.

Blue whales are the largest mammals on Earth. Their hearts are the same size as a small car and their tongues can weigh as much as an elephant. Blue whales are majestic creatures, but sadly they are an endangered species. There are only around 10 000 - 25 000 blue whales left in the wild, which is really sad.

Rewrite the extract above using only facts. Use an objective tone.

....

....

....

....

....

Blue Whales

5 These sentences are from another part of the report. Match the words and phrases to the sentences they have been removed from.

Blue whales communicate using low-pitched sounds.

Sound travels faster through water than air.

Other whales can hear the sounds but humans often can't.

Although it is the biggest, the blue whale is not the loudest.

- hear the sounds
- animal on earth
- with each other
- it travels through

6 Use the facts below to write a paragraph about blue whales for the report. Use an objective tone, technical terms and generalisations to make it sound reliable.

Facts about blue whales:
- Length: 24–33 meters
- Weight: 180 000 kilograms
- Top speed: 30 miles per hour
- Life span: 80-90 years
- They can't swallow anything larger than a grapefruit
- They can eat up to 40 million krill (tiny shellfish) a day

....
....
....
....
....
....
....
....

Now Try This Write a short report about a topic you are interested in, for example, a sport or an animal. Use an objective tone, technical terms and generalisations.

A King of the Past

Warm Up Question

1 Circle the noun phrase and underline the relative clause.

The ruby and sapphire necklace, which I bought, was missing.

2 This is an extract from a newspaper report. Tick the boxes next to the sentences that only have noun phrases underlined.

The Cooper family of Littlewick-on-Candle had their mealtime interrupted yesterday by a surprise guest. ☐

A tall man with a gleaming sword appeared at their door, dressed head-to-toe in authentic medieval armour. ☐

The man claimed to be the legendary British leader, King Arthur. ☐

Father Rob Cooper offered him a plate of sausages and mash. ☐

3 For each box below, write two different sentences by rearranging the sentence parts in different orders.

- before the family noticed
- Arthur knighted the cat

1 ....

2 ....

- in a fit of rage
- Arthur called the TV a witch

1 ....

2 ....

A King of the Past

4 Read this extract from the newspaper report. Fill in the gaps with relative clauses to give extra information about the underlined nouns.

The king then explained that he hadn't had a nap in over a century, so he went to sleep on the family's <u>sofa</u>, which ....

In the morning, <u>Benjamin</u>, who .... , took the king to a <u>cafe</u> that .... Eyewitnesses report that Arthur ate a small army of gingerbread men.

5 Rewrite the following sentences. Add a relative clause to each one and vary the structure of your sentences to make them interesting.

Arthur rode the horse around the town. Arthur attacked the dragon statue.

....

....

6 Continue the newspaper report, explaining why the Cooper family had to pick up King Arthur from the police station. Use varied sentence structures and include noun phrases and relative clauses.

....

....

....

....

....

....

 Write a short newspaper article about an unexpected visitor. Use relative clauses and noun phrases to add information, and vary the structure of your sentences.

Section Six — Non-Fiction

Letter to a Youth Group

Warm Up Question

  Circle the person below you would be most likely to send a formal letter to.

Your headteacher   Your best friend   Your parent

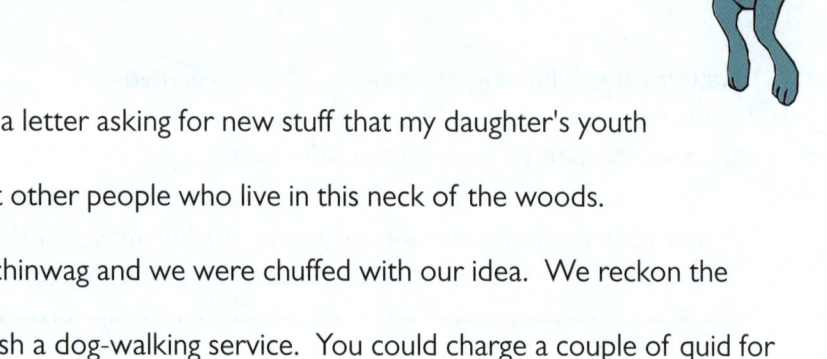

This is an extract from a letter to the leader of a local youth group. Underline all the informal words and phrases.

Dear Mrs Evans,

You recently sent a letter asking for new stuff that my daughter's youth group could do to benefit other people who live in this neck of the woods. My daughter and I had a chinwag and we were chuffed with our idea. We reckon the youth group could establish a dog-walking service. You could charge a couple of quid for people who live in the area, and also offer the service to the local dog shelter. Kids could go out in pairs to walk the dogs. I'm sure that most of your members would be up for this.

  Read the next part of the letter. Circle the correct options from the underlined words to make the letter formal.

I believe / guess that this service would be a proper / really good addition to the group's activities for several reasons. Firstly, it would encourage / kick-start young people's involvement in the community, which would improve the group's clout / reputation in the area. I am also firmly convinced that this activity would be a brilliant / cool chance for young people to rub shoulders / interact with a wide range of different people. In my opinion, your members would be able to learn loads / a great deal from others in the community if you decided to commence / kick off this dog-walking service.

Section Six — Non-Fiction

Letter to a Youth Group

4 Add a clause to each of these sentences from the letter to give extra information. Use formal language.

Furthermore, a dog-walking service would require young people to care for animals .... If you were to connect the service with the local dog shelter .... , the volunteers would also be helping to care for dogs that are in particular need of love and affection. This activity would be wonderful for everyone involved ....

5 The sentence below is the start of the letter's final paragraph. Complete the letter using formal language.

Lastly, I think that this service would be beneficial for young people's health.

....
....
....
....
....
....
....
....
....
....
....
....

Now Try This Write a letter to a local bakery, asking them to donate a prize for your school's raffle. Your letter should have at least three paragraphs and should use formal language.

Section Six — Non-Fiction

Section Seven — Fiction

The Dragon Rider

Warm Up Question

1 Circle the technique used in the sentence below.

The wind roared angrily around the tiny island, blasting it with frosty air.

(metaphor)   (simile)   (personification)

2 Read this extract from a fantasy story.
Underline the similes and circle the metaphors.

Bianca's eyes glinted like diamonds in the sunlight. Her smile was a crescent moon, and she trembled with excitement as she packed up her bag. Her stomach a twisted knot, she leapt out the door, as fierce and determined as a lion. Bianca started for the forest. This was it — she was going to ride a dragon for the first time.

Choose one metaphor or simile and explain what it shows about Bianca.

....

....

3 Draw a line from each of these sentences to the technique it uses.

Bianca's feet were wings as she flew through the silent forest.

Her hair streamed out behind her like a mighty knight's banner.

Branches waved as she ran through the trees, cheering her on in her quest.

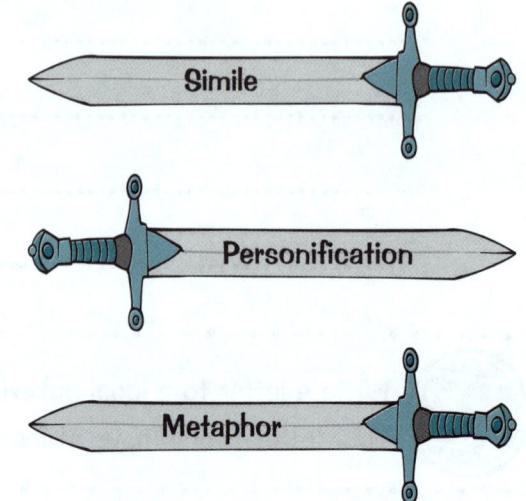

The Dragon Rider

4 Bianca reaches the dragon's cave and goes inside. Read the extract below and fill in the gaps, using appeals to the senses to describe the scene.

Appeals to the senses are descriptions of sight, hearing, touch, taste or smell.

She crept along the ………………………… tunnel which led to the dragon's lair. The ground was …………………………, and her hands grazed ………………………… rocks when she reached out to stop herself from falling. As she edged along the passage, the air became warmer. The scent of ………………………… in the air made her stifle a cough, and a ………………………… noise told Bianca that the dragon was close.

5 Bianca sees the dragon sitting on a pile of treasure. Using personification, rewrite the sentences below to describe the scene.

The shiny coins fell to the ground.

………………………………………………………………………………………………

The chest full of gold was in the corner.

………………………………………………………………………………………………

A small fire lit the cave.

………………………………………………………………………………………………

6 Bianca climbs onto the dragon's back and they fly out of the cave. Write a description of Bianca and what she sees. Use similes, metaphors and appeals to the senses.

………………………………………………………………………………………………
………………………………………………………………………………………………
………………………………………………………………………………………………
………………………………………………………………………………………………
………………………………………………………………………………………………

Now Try This Write a description of the following places that Bianca and the dragon visit:
a witch's castle   an enormous lake   an icy mountain

Section Seven — Fiction

Far from Rome

Warm Up Question

1) What is the atmosphere of a text?

The way it looks. ☐   The way it feels. ☐   The way it sounds. ☐

2) Read this extract from a story about a young Roman soldier.

Justus gazed, open-mouthed, at the mass of soldiers gathered on the beaches, sunlight glinting off their bright shields. This was it — he had finally reached the very fringes of the Roman Empire. His mind filled with wonderful images of the daring, exciting adventures he knew he would have. He could hardly wait to begin the journey through Britain.

The soldiers around him felt differently. Sweat glistened on their foreheads and their legs trembled. They stared at the landscape as though it were a dark and terrible omen.

Fill in the table to describe what atmosphere each example creates.

Example	What atmosphere it creates
daring, exciting adventures	
a dark and terrible omen	

3) Read the next part of the story below. Underline the verbs, adjectives and adverbs that create a dangerous atmosphere.

Icy rain stabbed at his face as the army marched down the long road. The ground was perilously muddy, and his feet kept slipping from beneath him. Justus could hardly see, but the hairs on the back of his neck prickled with nervous energy. Thunder rumbled ominously through the ebony sky, and Justus gulped. A flash of lightning illuminated rows of sinister trees in the distance. He couldn't wait to arrive at their camp.

Section Seven — Fiction

Far from Rome

4 Justus and his legion arrive at their camp as night falls. Fill in the gaps with adjectives and adverbs so that the extract has a positive atmosphere.

Justus had never felt so .... to

.... stop marching and sit down. He wiped his

.... forehead and looked around. The sight of

the tiny port gave his .... body a fresh burst

of energy. A .... orange light blinked from

the top of a lighthouse, guiding ships .... to

the shore. The long, straight road that stretched out towards the

.... town looked ....

The place seemed to promise refuge, and Justus gave a

.... smile. He would .... rest

his head here tonight.

5 Rewrite the extract above to give it a mysterious atmosphere. You can change the extract as much as you want.

....
....
....
....
....
....
....

After resting for the night, Justus and his legion begin to prepare for battle. Finish the story, using description to create a tense atmosphere.

Section Seven — Fiction

A Bumpy Ride

Warm Up Question

1 Underline the contracted forms below. Then circle any other informal language.

"Woah! Where's Alex? I can't wait to show her — she'll be gobsmacked!"

2 Read this extract from a story about two friends visiting a theme park. Then complete the task below.

"Can you believe that we're finally here?" asked Imogen. She bounced on her toes as she looked at the queue. "I can't wait to get inside!"

"Yeah, I suppose," Hiro replied tensely. He avoided her eyes.

Imogen nudged Hiro and gave him a reassuring smile. "You'll love it once we're on the rides," she said. She'd been telling him that for weeks now.

"I really hope so," Hiro said quietly, a slight tremble in his voice.

Write an example of each character's dialogue in the table below. Then explain what the example shows you about that person.

Character	Example	What it shows
Hiro		
Imogen		

3 In the next part of the story, Hiro and Imogen enter the theme park. The underlined words create two different types of atmosphere for the extract. Decide what atmosphere you want the extract to have and circle the appropriate options.

"There are no / so many people here!" Imogen exclaimed.

"It's a bit eerie / crowded, don't you think?" asked Hiro. "I thought that it would be busier / quieter than this. I don't really like it."

"It makes me feel strange / more excited," said Imogen enthusiastically / nervously. "It's like we've walked into a graveyard / party."

Section Seven — Fiction

A Bumpy Ride

4 Hiro and Imogen explore the theme park and decide which ride to go on first. Rewrite the extract below using dialogue to move the story forward.

Imogen wanted to go on the enormous roller coaster. Hiro refused to go on it. He looked at the map and suggested a quiet boat ride instead. Imogen scoffed and said it was boring. Then she spotted the ghost train, and insisted that they try that.

....

....

....

....

....

....

5 Hiro and Imogen are riding the ghost train when it breaks down. Continue the story, using dialogue to develop their characters, create an atmosphere and advance the action.

....

....

....

....

....

....

....

....

....

Now Try This — Write a short story about two friends visiting a chocolate factory. Use dialogue to develop your characters, create an exciting atmosphere and move the plot forward.

Beneath the Stones

Warm Up Question

1 Place the events below in chronological order by labelling them 1-3.

.... The bird lays eggs.   .... The bird hatches.   .... The bird grows up.

2 Below are the parts of a story set in modern England. Put the parts into a logical order by writing letters on the timeline.

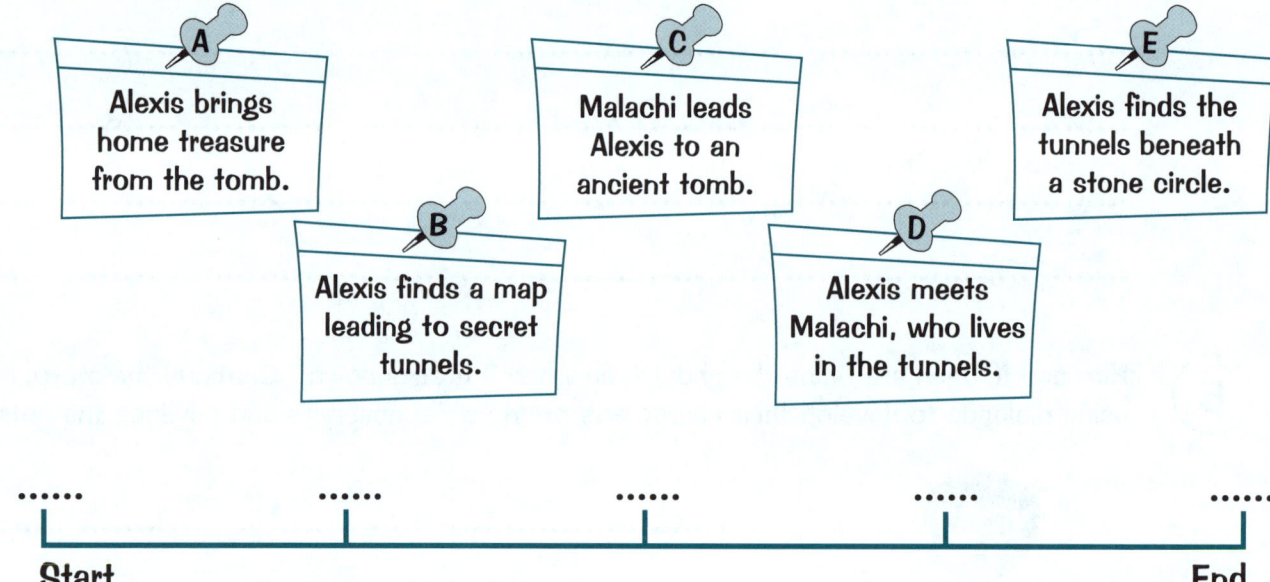

- **A** Alexis brings home treasure from the tomb.
- **B** Alexis finds a map leading to secret tunnels.
- **C** Malachi leads Alexis to an ancient tomb.
- **D** Alexis meets Malachi, who lives in the tunnels.
- **E** Alexis finds the tunnels beneath a stone circle.

Start .... End

3 In this part of the story, Alexis has been exploring the tunnels for several days, and is starting to regret his journey. Explain why you think the writer included this flashback.

Shivering in the dark, Alexis's mind started to wander. He recalled the day when he found the map. He was strolling through the woods in July: the world was green and yellow, and warm sunlight trickled through the idle leaves, casting shifting patterns on his skin. His eyes caught on something glinting in a pile of leaves and he gasped — it was like nothing he'd seen before... In the tunnels, Alexis's eyes snapped open. He didn't have time to daydream.

Think about how the flashback makes you feel.

....
....

Beneath the Stones

4 Later in the story, Alexis's torch has broken and he is starting to worry. Fill in the table with the cliffhanger from the extract, and explain how it makes you feel.

Alexis lit a match, casting dancing shadows across the walls of the tunnel. Something brushed Alexis's skin — it felt like a ghostly wind. But that was impossible: this far into the tunnels, the air was thick and motionless like syrup. His breathing felt heavy. Suddenly, he heard footsteps padding softly behind him.

Cliffhanger	How it makes you feel

5 The footsteps belong to Malachi, who leads Alexis through the tunnels to a burial chamber filled with treasure. Finish the story, including a flashback and a cliffhanger.

Malachi was tall and wiry, and he had to stoop even here, where the roof of the tunnel was high. "Not far to go," he said with a toothy grin, beckoning Alexis onwards.

....

....

....

....

....

....

....

 Alexis realises the map has a torn edge, and there is a missing section. Write the first three paragraphs of Alexis's search for the rest of the map, ending with a cliffhanger.

Section Seven — Fiction

The Animals of the Rainforest

Warm Up Question

1 Circle all the words that rhyme.

doubt   boat   float   code   groan   wrote

2 Read this poem about a sloth and underline the alliteration.

A baby sloth is born on high,
Where leaves flutter and branches sigh,
And passion flowers grin and grow,
While fireflies flicker to join the show.

As it scrunches its simple, smiling face,
The baby sloth moves at a pitiful pace.
It slowly descends the tallest of trees,
And reaches the roots at the age of three.

3 This is an extract from a different poem. Add your own alliteration to the couplets below.

The jaguar .... stalks its prey,

But .... Benjamin scares it away.

Squirrel monkeys .... and swing,

They .... and laugh at everything.

The .... toucan glides through the clouds,

Then chirps a .... song out loud.

Imagery is language that creates a picture in your head. This includes similes and metaphors.

4 Add imagery to the gaps below to complete each sentence.

The frog's skin was as orange as ....

The snake coiled around the branch like ....

The boar was ....

The waterfall roared as loudly as ....

Section Seven — Fiction

The Animals of the Rainforest

5 Read the poem below and circle the onomatopoeic words.

The song of the forest is loud and constant,
It buzzes by night and rumbles all day long.
And even in peaceful and secluded spots,
The hummingbirds' wings are flapping away.

Continue the poem above. Use onomatopoeia to create a busy atmosphere.

....

....

....

....

6 Read the poem below and underline all the rhyming words. Write a poem that has the same rhyme scheme and the same number of beats per line.

Mister Macaw, why are they bright?
Your feathers — yellow, red and blue.
Treetop dweller, give me an answer!
Why do you look the way you do?

....

....

....

....

 Write a short poem about each of the following animals: turtle, scorpion, anteater. Use a different rhyme scheme and number of beats per line for each animal's poem.

Section Seven — Fiction

End of Year Test

Read the text, then answer the questions that follow.
In the extract, Tom is exploring his aunt and uncle's house at nighttime.

Extract from *Tom's Midnight Garden*

He moved down the hall to the door at its far end. It was a door he had never seen opened — the Kitsons used the door at the front. They said that the door at the back was only a less convenient way to the street, through a back-yard — a strip of paving where dustbins were kept and where the tenants of the ground-floor back flat garaged their car under a tarpaulin*.

5   Never having had occasion to use the door, Tom had no idea how it might be secured at night. If it were locked, and the key kept elsewhere... But it was not locked, he found; only bolted. He drew the bolt and, very slowly, to make no sound, turned the door-knob.

Hurry! whispered the house; and the grandfather clock at the heart of it beat an anxious tick, tick.

10   Tom opened the door wide and let in the moonlight. It flooded in, as bright as daylight — the white daylight that comes before the full rising of the sun. The illumination was perfect, but Tom did not at once turn to see what it showed him of the clock-face. Instead he took a step forward on to the doorstep. He was staring, at first in surprise, then with indignation, at what he saw outside. That they should have deceived him — lied to him — like this! They had said, 'It's

15   not worth your while going out at the back, Tom.' So carelessly they had described it: 'A sort of back-yard, very poky, with rubbish bins. Really, there's nothing to see.'

Nothing... Only this: a great lawn where flower-beds bloomed; a towering fir-tree, and thick, beetle-browed yews that humped their shapes down two sides of the lawn; on the third side, to the right, a greenhouse almost the size of a real house; from each corner of the lawn, a path that

20   twisted away to some other depths of garden, with other trees.

Tom had stepped forward instinctively, catching his breath in surprise; now he let his breath out in a deep sigh. He would steal out here tomorrow, by daylight. They had tried to keep this from him, but they could not stop him now — not his aunt, nor his uncle, nor the back flat tenants, nor even particular Mrs Bartholomew. He would run full tilt over the grass, leaping the flower-beds; he

25   would peer through the glittering panes of the greenhouse — perhaps open the door and go in; he would visit each alcove and archway clipped in the yew-trees — he would climb the trees and make his way from one to another through thickly interlacing branches. When they came calling him, he would hide, silent and safe as a bird, among this richness of leaf and bough and tree-trunk.

By Philippa Pearce

Glossary
tarpaulin — a waterproof cloth

End of Year Test

1. Look at lines 5-9. How does the author suggest that Tom is doing something that he shouldn't be?

....

....
2 marks

2. Name the technique that the writer uses in line 8.

....
1 mark

3. Circle the word which would best replace "indignation" (line 13).

wonder   excitement   anger   anxiety
1 mark

4. Which verb from lines 21-25 means 'to move secretly'?

....
1 mark

5. Write down two things that Tom wants to do in the garden.

....

....
2 marks

6. Do you think that the garden is impressive? Give reasons for your answer.

....

....
2 marks

7. What impression of Tom do you get from this extract? Explain your answer.

....

....
2 marks

End of Year Test

8 Circle the clauses and underline the phrases.

Mia goes swimming   little slimy snails   those fluffy clouds

the tree over there   wishes can come true   we enjoy biking

6 marks

9 Write a sentence with each set of words, using an apostrophe to show possession.

Nico   red   scarf   ....

dark   cavern   bat   ....

giraffes   vanished   spots   ....

3 marks

10 Fill in the gaps in the sentences below using the correct words from the box.

tale / tail   soul / sole   throne / thrown

The .... of my shoe made a pattern in the snow.

Many kings have sat on that grand, golden ....

The old man told us an exciting .... about a brave warrior.

3 marks

11 Write 'A' next to the active sentence and 'P' next to the passive sentence. Then, label the underlined part of each sentence as either subject or object.

The bedroom was decorated. ☐   The snake shed its skin. ☐

....

2 marks

End of Year Test

12 Punctuate the following sentences correctly.

I bought three flavours of ice cream toffee mint and vanilla .

Before I could eat it a seagull which was hungry stole it .

Feeling annoyed I shouted loudly Buy your own you greedy bird

3 marks

13 Add your own adjectives and adverbs to the passage below.

Elise and Imran tiptoed .... into the haunted house. They could dimly make out a .... staircase and spiders studying them .... from the roof, some dangling down on cobwebs. "This is ....," whispered Imran, looking .... at Elise.

5 marks

14 Tick the two sentences which are in the present progressive.

We were collecting beetles. ☐   They are climbing a tree. ☐

Mariko is cartwheeling. ☐   Xander was eating toast. ☐

2 marks

Rewrite the sentences that you ticked so they are in the past progressive.

....

....

2 marks

15 Write the correct spellings of these words on the lines.

benefitial → ....

important → ....

probibly → ....

emergancy → ....

4 marks

End of Year Test

16 Circle the correct linking word or phrase to make the text flow.

Millions of years ago, dinosaurs roamed the Earth. However / Therefore, these creatures went extinct. A larger crater has been discovered, so / because some scientists believe the dinosaurs were killed by a meteor, whereas / since others think their extinction was caused by a volcanic eruption.

3 marks

17 Fill in the gaps with the word type in brackets so that the extract has an exciting atmosphere.

When Katie saw the carefully wrapped box, she .... (verb) out of her chair. .... (adverb), she tore the paper off the present and opened the lid. When she looked inside and saw the box's .... (adjective) contents, she .... (verb). "A scooter!" she cried .... (adverb). "I can't believe it!"

5 marks

18 Rewrite these sentences to include the techniques in the box.

The blanket was soft.   [simile]

....

The star shot across the sky.   [metaphor]

....

The wind blew through my hair.   [an appeal to the senses]

....

3 marks

End of Year Test

End of Year Test

19 Rewrite the following opinions as facts. Use an objective tone.

I thought climbing Mount Everest was difficult.

....

Nia believes that spider monkeys can grab things with their tails.

....

2 marks

20 Write a cliffhanger ending to the following extract. Vary the structure of your sentences to make them interesting.

Paula heard a noise in the shed. Slowly, she opened the door and peered inside. Near the wall, she spotted a creature. The creature waved and giggled as it looked at Paula.

....

....

....

....

2 marks

21 Underline the alliteration and circle the onomatopoeic words in the poem below.

The cowboy's best horse, Jittery Jim,
Was far too scared to ever dare swim.
Along the shore, he strolled and he clipped.
Then, without warning, he slid and slipped.
Hearing Jim make a tremendous splash,
The cowboy heaved Jim out in a flash.

5 marks

Write two more lines to continue the poem above.
Use the same rhyme scheme and number of beats per line.

....

....

2 marks

Score: ☐ /63

Glossary

Abstract noun	A name for an idea or feeling, e.g. anger, beauty, curiosity.
Active sentence	A sentence where the subject does something to the object, e.g. Roshani played the guitar.
Adjective	A word that describes a noun, e.g. tiny hamster, hungry cat.
Adverb	A word that describes a verb, an adjective or other adverbs, e.g. sleepily, bravely, sometimes.
Adverbial	A group of words that behaves like an adverb.
Alliteration	When words begin with the same sound, e.g. The boy binned his bag.
Antonyms	Words that mean the opposite, e.g. big and small.
Audience	The person or people who the text is aimed at.
Clause	Part of a sentence that contains a subject and a verb.
Concrete noun	A name for a thing that you can see, touch, smell or hear, e.g. cat, egg.
Conjunction	A word or phrase that joins two parts of a sentence, e.g. I eat sausages and I eat chips.
Co-ordinating conjunction	A word that joins two main clauses in a sentence, e.g. and, but.
Determiner	Tells you whether a noun is general or specific, e.g. They baked a cake. They baked that cake.
First person	Used to write from the point of view of the writer, e.g. I sold my car.
Fronted adverbial	An adverbial that goes at the front of a sentence, e.g. After that, we went home.
Generalisation	Something that is true in most cases, e.g. Most lizards lay eggs.
Homophones	Words that sound the same but have a different meaning, e.g. I and eye.
Linking word or phrase	A word or phrase used to link two clauses, sentences or paragraphs, e.g. also, because, moreover.
Main clause	A clause that makes sense on its own, e.g. I read a book while I wait.
Metaphor	Describes something by saying it is something else, e.g. The classroom is a zoo.
Modal verb	Can show how likely something is, e.g. It might be sunny today.
Noun	A word that names something, e.g. banana, Tamar, Paris.
Noun phrase	A group of words containing a noun and any words describing the noun, e.g. the lazy lion.
Object	The person or thing in a sentence that has a verb done to it, e.g. The cat drinks the milk.

Glossary

Glossary

Onomatopoeia	When a word <u>sounds</u> like the thing it is describing, e.g. <u>crash</u>, <u>pop</u>.
Passive sentence	A sentence where something is <u>done to</u> the <u>subject</u>, e.g. <u>The guitar</u> was played by Roshani.
Past perfect	Used to talk about things that happened <u>before now</u>, and <u>before something else</u> happened, e.g. Jim <u>had spilt</u> his juice <u>when</u> Kaz arrived.
Past progressive	Used to show an action <u>was happening</u>, e.g. He <u>was licking</u> a stamp.
Personification	Using <u>human qualities</u> to <u>describe</u> something that's not human, e.g. The old chair <u>groaned</u> when he sat in it.
Preposition	Tells you <u>where</u>, <u>when</u> or <u>why</u> something happens, e.g. The bank is <u>next to</u> the post office.
Present perfect	Used to talk about things that <u>have already happened</u>, e.g. She <u>has seen</u> three films this week.
Present progressive	Used to show an action is <u>currently happening</u>, e.g. He <u>is driving</u> a car.
Pronoun	A word used to replace a noun, e.g. <u>I</u>, <u>he</u>, <u>she</u>, <u>they</u>.
Proper noun	A <u>name</u> for a particular <u>person</u>, <u>place</u> or <u>thing</u>, e.g. Rome, Tina, July.
Purpose	The <u>reason</u> for writing a text, e.g. to <u>persuade</u>, to <u>entertain</u>.
Relative clause	A <u>subordinate clause</u> that tells you more about a noun. It is often introduced by a <u>relative pronoun</u>, e.g. This is the cake <u>which I bought</u>.
Reported speech	What someone has said, but <u>not</u> in their <u>own words</u>.
Rhetorical question	A question that doesn't need an answer, e.g. Shouldn't we be protecting endangered species?
Simile	When you say one thing is <u>like</u> another, e.g. The clouds were <u>like sheep</u>.
Simple past	Used to write about things that have <u>already</u> happened, e.g. I <u>played</u> football yesterday.
Simple present	Used to write about things that are <u>happening now</u>, e.g. I <u>throw</u> the ball.
Standard English	English that follows the <u>rules</u> of spelling, punctuation and grammar.
Subject	The <u>person</u> or <u>thing</u> in a sentence <u>doing</u> a verb, e.g. <u>Neil</u> skipped home.
Subjunctive form	A verb form that appears in <u>formal</u> writing, e.g. I wish I <u>were</u> there.
Subordinate clause	A clause that <u>doesn't make sense</u> on its own, e.g. I read a book <u>while I wait for the bus</u>.
Subordinating conjunction	A word or phrase which joins a <u>main clause</u> to a <u>subordinate clause</u>, e.g. <u>when</u>, <u>because</u>.
Synonyms	Words that mean the same, e.g. <u>happy</u> and <u>joyful</u>.
Verb	A doing or being word, e.g. <u>talk</u>, <u>listen</u>, <u>hold</u>, <u>be</u>.

Answers

Pages 2-5 – Starter Test

1. "as quickly as meteors flash through the night sky" or "drooping in the saddle like a wilted flower" *(1 mark)*
2. E.g. captivating
   E.g. To emphasise how Melusina's beauty is so unusual that it seems magical *(1 mark for a sensible adjective, 1 mark for a sensible explanation)*
3. E.g. The fields in his kingdom "flourished".
   He gained the reputation of a "mighty leader".
   (1 mark for each correct answer)
4. E.g. No. The count promised that he would "never attempt to" see Melusina on Saturdays and he broke this promise.
   (1 mark for any sensible answer and 1 mark for any sensible explanation)
5. E.g. I think he was heartbroken. He had "lived happily" and been "in love" with Melusina, so her disappearance would have upset him. *(1 mark for any sensible answer, 1 mark for any sensible explanation)*
6. You should have circled:
   distant, cosy, uncomfortable
   You should have underlined:
   calmly, slowly, often
   (1 mark for each correct adjective or adverb)
7. Allison (who likes exercise) is running a marathon in November.
   The mountain (which is difficult to climb) is covered in snow.
   (1 mark for each correct sentence)
8. We made an agreement to visit the treehouse on Friday.
   The villain claimed that he was totally invincible.
   Winning the talent show was a memorable event.
   (1 mark for each correct answer)
9. Despite not knowing the way, I led the group onwards.
   All of the donkeys started braying while I was at the farm.
   (1 mark for each correct answer)
10. "A raccoon is in my bin!" Frank shouted.
    Isla moaned, "Why did my umbrella break?"
    (1 mark for each correctly punctuated sentence)
11. Open *(1 mark)*
12. Leah said she wouldn't be scared if the volcano erupted.
    Jade told me that the festival starts tomorrow.
    (1 mark for each correct sentence)
13. Thunder grumbled loudly overhead. — personification
    The sheet of ice was a mirror. — metaphor
    The cat's eyes sparkled like jewels. — simile
    (1 mark for each correct answer)
14. E.g. Who wouldn't want to visit this safari park?
    E.g. This safari is to die for!
    (1 mark for each sensible answer)

Page 6 – Nouns and Adjectives

1. be
2. E.g. The pie wouldn't fit in the new oven.
   The pride of hungry lions had never seen a shoe before.
   The light of fireflies filled the gloomy cave.
3. You should have underlined:
   crowd, air, singer, stage, song, audience, tune, singer, stage
   You should have circled:
   joy, feeling, anticipation, silence, confidence
4. E.g. Erica looked outside and saw a sky full of angry clouds and pouring rain above the small town where she lived.
5. We grew beautiful flowers.
   He bought an expensive teapot.

Page 7 – Verbs and Adverbs

1. Alex never speaks and eats at the same time.
   I always love visiting my friend's house, and I never want to leave.
2. E.g. The tortoise played jazz impressively on the keyboard.
   The aliens danced happily for six hours and then flew back to their planet.
   Rita carefully waters her flowers every morning.
3. Josh angrily snapped his pencil in half.
   Maybe Chanti will win the top prize in the raffle.
   Perhaps everyone found the film hard to understand.
4. Alana wouldn't want a new bag, even if she could afford one.
   You should really try the chocolate cake — it's delicious.
   I might start taking piano lessons, if I had the time.

Now Try This:
E.g. Rebecca swam gracefully across the pool.
Adam looked at the camera shyly.
Mitch stormed out of the tent loudly.

Page 8 – Synonyms and Antonyms

1. You should have underlined: hot / cold.
   You should have circled: complex / complicated.
2. loud — quiet
   up — down
   end — start
3. Any suitable synonyms. For example:
   strange — weird, huge — massive, funny — hilarious, brilliant — amazing, furious — angry, easy — effortless, scream — screech, scared — afraid, leap — jump, gaze — stare
4. Across:
   1. right, 4. amused, 6. large, 7. shrink
   Down:
   1. rise, 2. tall, 3. love, 4. after, 5. truth

Page 9 – Pronouns

1. That idea was mine — don't copy me.
   Alice knew she had a good chance of winning.
2. Havva and her little sister Ayse couldn't wait. First, their dad bought the tickets and handed Havva hers. Then, they saw an enormous roller coaster. The people on the ride screamed with joy — as they reached the top, all of them let out a huge shriek which echoed through the fairground.
3. My brother Rupert loves to destroy furniture. He annoys my mum a lot. She gets angry and calls him lots of names. One time, he shredded a cushion which was hers. Later, she invited her friend Priya around, whose dog Nibbles helped Rupert tear down the curtains.

Now Try This:
E.g. Have you seen a dog that can talk?
That's the woman whose album I bought.
This is the book which he gave me.
We are looking for the person whose car this is.
Have they said who will be on their team?

Answers

Page 10 – Clauses and Phrases

1. <u>When I was a pirate</u>, I had a parrot called Gary.
   <u>Although I do not understand chess</u>, I managed to beat my dad.
   She speaks perfect French, <u>even though she has never visited France</u>.
   <u>If you start swimming now</u>, you will reach Greenland by Christmas.
   Luke always sang pop songs <u>when he was alone</u>.

2. Any suitable relative clauses. For example:
   The toddler, <u>who was only three</u>, wasn't great at darts.
   I found a ladder, <u>which reached the clouds</u>, and began to climb.
   Tavan, <u>who had been waiting a long time</u>, dived into the pool.
   The shop, <u>which sold chocolate</u>, was closed.
   Annie begged her mum, <u>who disliked pets</u>, to buy a dog.
   I saw the snow, <u>which covered the whole garden</u>, and jumped for joy.

3. the scuba diver <u>with her pet fish</u>
   her favourite recipe <u>from Greece</u>
   a huge mountain <u>near the lake</u>
   the beautiful fountain pen <u>on the table</u>

4. Any suitable prepositional phrase. For example:
   the nasty vampire <u>with a taste for garlic</u>
   a long-lost necklace <u>in the attic</u>

Now Try This:
E.g. Robin Hood, <u>who stole from the rich</u>, gave to the poor.
Oliver, <u>who was very hungry</u>, asked for more food.
Dorothy, <u>who had a dog called Toto</u>, defeated the witch.

Page 11 – Prepositions and Determiners

1. You should have circled: beneath
   You should have underlined: those

2. E.g. The computer is <u>on</u> the desk.
   The keyboard is <u>beside</u> the printer.
   The picture is <u>above</u> the keyboard.
   The chair is <u>in front of</u> the desk.
   The books are leaning <u>against</u> the wall.

3. This apple came from <u>their</u> garden.
   There are <u>few</u> things I like less than broccoli.
   There are some biscuits left, but there aren't <u>many</u> cakes left.

4. E.g. I bought some apples and a banana before lunch.
   These trees fell down because of the storm.

Page 12 – Conjunctions

1. Drew parked his scooter <u>before</u> he entered the ice cream shop. He had been here many times, <u>yet</u> the sight still took his breath away. The tubs of ice cream sparkled <u>as</u> the sun shone through the window. <u>Although</u> he was hungry, he wanted to keep staring forever, bathed in the window's glow.

2. I tried to put on a magic show for our class, <u>but</u> it went terribly. I wanted to start with a card trick, <u>so</u> I asked Michael to pick a card. Somehow, I managed to guess the wrong card, <u>even though</u> I did everything correctly. Then, I tried to pull my rabbit Tricksy out of my hat, but she was shy <u>because</u> the whole class was giggling. She jumped out of my hat <u>and</u> ran into the toilets.

3. E.g. It was a sunny day when we went on the school trip.
   We visited the harbour and I saw three porpoises playing.
   No one else saw them so I felt very lucky.

Now Try This:
'before' is a conjunction in the sentence 'The cat left before I could stop it.' because it joins together a main clause and a subordinate clause.

Page 13 – Present and Past Tense

1. ran, ate, went

2. My aunt sends me letters from Singapore.
   Bobby leaves the house to go to school.

3. I <u>hopped</u> to school on one foot because I lost a bet.
   Shauna <u>wondered</u> what to do with her spare paint.
   The bus <u>stopped</u> in front of the castle.
   Amrit <u>went</u> to a golf club after school.
   Andrew's bike tyre <u>burst</u>.

4. E.g. The man looks in the mirror with surprise.
   The man looked in the mirror and was surprised.

Page 14 – Present and Past Progressive

1. The architect <u>is</u> drawing a blueprint.
   The scarecrow <u>is</u> playing a banjo.
   I <u>am</u> baking a chocolate cake.

2. E.g. Alison was rollerskating to school.
   The otter was eating a fish.
   Ryan was fishing that day.

3.

verb	present progressive	past progressive
to swim	Dolly <u>is swimming</u> alone.	Dolly <u>was swimming</u> alone.
to learn	The driver <u>is learning</u> fast.	The driver <u>was learning</u> fast.
to eat	Paula <u>is eating</u> her meal.	Paula <u>was eating</u> her meal.
to take	She <u>is taking</u> the exam.	She <u>was taking</u> the exam.
to think	I <u>am thinking</u> about sweets.	I <u>was thinking</u> about sweets.

Now Try This:
E.g. Last week, I was planning to go to the shops. I was doing my homework. I was trying to ride a bike.
Last year, I was preparing to go camping. I was growing my hair long. I was practising my yo-yo skills.

Page 15 – The Perfect Form

1. had

2. The car had started to rust.
   I had used up all my ink.

3. Mrs Stevens <u>had dropped</u> her books.
   The taxi <u>had parked</u> outside my house.
   I <u>had won</u> the game at the last moment.
   Arjun <u>had visited</u> Adam's house before school.
   Misty <u>had eaten</u> a lot of marshmallows.

4. Eric has opened his lunch box. Eric has told his dad repeatedly that he doesn't like egg sandwiches, but his dad has packed them anyway.

Page 16 – Subject and Object

1. E.g. <u>The stegosaurus</u> fell asleep.
   Macy loves her new <u>dress</u>.
   The tiny <u>dog</u> growls at Finley.
   <u>Sharon</u> stood on the sand, shouting at the ocean.

2. In the sentences below, the subject is in **bold** and the object is underlined.
   The air steward broke <u>the chair</u>.
   The owl flies over <u>the barn</u>.
   Two days ago, **Aaron** hosted <u>a party</u>.

Answers

Carys enjoyed <u>the view</u> from her room.
Kala bought <u>a phone</u> in town.
Satisifed, **Talia** ran <u>home</u> happily.
The shopkeeper closes <u>his shop</u>.
Will left <u>his book</u> at the beach.

3. E.g. The boy eats the carrot.
   The frog watches the tadpole.
   Kerry high-fives Ahmed.

Now Try This:
E.g. Timothy dropped Rana.
Rana almost drops Timothy.

Page 17 – Passive and Active

1. You should have circled: The string was chased by the cat.
   You should have underlined: The cat chased the string.
2. The ball was thrown by Ali.
   The table was built by Mum.
3. They were asked if they wanted popcorn.
   Luca was bored by the trailers.
   Then he was told off by an usher.
4. Uncle Tim thanked Jordan.
   Northstone FC won the match.
   The dog chased the man.

Page 18 – Standard and Non-Standard English

1. I didn't see nothing. — N
   Beth and Izzy haven't met before. — S
   I could of helped you. — N
   Molly's done lots of paintings. — S
2. Raul <u>saw</u> you at the restaurant.
   They <u>came</u> to our house recently.
   She <u>isn't</u> going to play with us.
3. I won't sing no song. — Double negative
   I don't like that shirt at all. — Single negative
   Chocolate won't do you no good. — Double negative
   I can't find my books nowhere. — Double negative
4. They were losing in the first half, but then they scored.
   I haven't seen Clare since Rachel and I went to her house.

Now Try This:
E.g. The word "them" in this sentence is non-Standard English because "them" is a pronoun, not a determiner.

Page 19 – Formal and Informal Language

1. father, money, receive
2. E.g. I cannot attend your birthday party because I have a family event.
   To be truthful, I am feeling quite unwell.
   Is she a famous footballer?
3. It is crucial that you be awake at all times.
   If I were the Queen, I would abolish Mondays.
4. If I <u>were</u> alone, I would read a book.
   She proposes that you <u>write</u> the play.
   It is essential that the class <u>be</u> quiet during this presentation.
   I wouldn't eat that if I <u>were</u> you.
   The King insists that all swords <u>be</u> sheathed immediately.

Page 20-21 – Grammar Practice

1. E.g. The <u>woman</u> is <u>tired</u>.
   The <u>leaves</u> looked <u>brown</u>.
2. I went out to see the night sky with my older brother. Astronomy is his hobby — <u>he</u> knows a lot about planets and stars. We climbed to the top of a hill. I didn't have a telescope so he let me use <u>his</u>. Suddenly, another stargazer shouted. <u>She</u> could see Jupiter in her telescope. <u>We</u> all took turns to look and it was amazing.
3. Any suitable synonyms and antonyms. E.g.
   danger: synonym — peril
           antonym — safety
   perfect: synonym — flawless
            antonym — imperfect
   skilful: synonym — talented
            antonym — inept
4. E.g. I was tired, <u>so</u> I lay down.
   Chloe likes pears, <u>but</u> she hates apples.
5. Danielle, who was afraid of the dark, kept her night light on. — R
   They discovered the mouse that had been eating all of the flour. — M
   The tennis stadium, which was open-air, was flooded by the rain. — R
6. We <u>were</u> there last year, and we <u>saw</u> Lydia's family.
   You should <u>have</u> asked who <u>did</u> it.
   My cousins <u>were</u> in the shop but they didn't see <u>anything</u>.
7. Dad cooks fish fingers on Fridays — simple present
   I have seen that film twice — present perfect
   This time last year, we were exploring Mexico City — past progressive
   I had just discovered a treasure map — past perfect
8. The head teacher requests that parents be present at the meeting.
9. My team played a game of football. I scored a goal.

Now Try This:
E.g. My captain clapped me on the back. She said she was really proud of me. Even though I am the youngest, I am the best player on our team.
The rest of the match was exciting. The other team scored again to draw level. Then, at the last minute, our captain headed the ball and scored an amazing goal. We won the match against the league champions!

Page 22 – Sentence Punctuation

1. E.g. To start a sentence.
   To start a proper noun.
   To use the pronoun 'I'.
2. False
3. I wanted to go to the zoo but William didn't.
4. <u>Alec</u> had two guinea pigs called <u>Popcorn</u> and <u>Scrapper</u>.
   <u>Padma</u> is going to stay in <u>Cornwall</u> next <u>March</u>.
5. Do you like apples — ?
   That's incredible — !
   This film is terrifying — !
   Don't sit there — !
   Shall we ride our bikes — ?
   Have you seen my sock — ?
6. E.g. Where is the music classroom<u>?</u>
   This is the best day ever<u>!</u>

Page 23 – Commas in Lists

1. Hannah's best friends are called Meena, Tina and Sabrina.
   Timon has posters of pop stars, footballers and dragons on his wall.

Answers

2. The octopus had many legs, a hat and a worried look.
   My sister likes football, hockey, swimming and running.
   Jess had a party with lots of games, a magician and a bouncy castle.
   Nadia's three brothers are called Hari, Umar and Malik.
   I got two board games, three books and some chocolate for Christmas.

3. E.g. My favourite hobbies are badminton, kayaking, reading and chess.
   My best friend has a dog, a cat, a gerbil and two hamsters.
   I would like to visit Italy, Japan, Nigeria and Ireland.

Now Try This:
E.g. Last Saturday, I stayed at home. I played video games, ate nice food, rested and spoke to my friends on the phone. On Sunday, I went to the mountains and did lots of outdoor activities like hiking, skiing, snowboarding and climbing.

Page 24 — Commas After Subordinate Clauses

1. Although Kim enjoys swimming, she doesn't like the sea.
   When I am older, I'll write a book about my life.

2. Although she's small, Harriet's very good at basketball.
   Before we go home, let's go to the park.
   When their dad arrived, Mo and Kit hid in the bushes.
   After 'Talented Elephants' finishes, we'll watch 'Dogs Ahoy'.

3. Until the food arrives, I will be hungry.
   As she was on holiday, Samara stayed up late.
   Unless you like cats, you shouldn't go there.

Now Try This:
E.g. Because my surname starts with 'Z', I am always last in the register.
As it's your birthday, I've made you a chocolate cake.
Unless you train regularly, you will struggle with cross-country running.

Page 25 — Commas After Fronted Adverbials

1. In September, we are going to Florida.

2. Twice a week, I play tiddlywinks.
   At the back of the drawer, you'll find the forks.
   After an hour, Suzie went home.

3. In Spain, we went windsurfing three times.
   With a cackle of glee, the witch vanished.
   Before dinner, Rowan went for a bike ride.
   On Tuesday afternoon, we're going skating.
   Last night, Zoe read a book in her armchair.

4. E.g. Next year, we will move to Scotland.
   On Saturday mornings, I get up early for orchestra.
   At the end of the road, there is an abandoned house.
   In London, Gabriel went to Hyde Park.

Page 26 — Commas For Extra Information

1. The pigsty, which is next to the stable, always smells bad.
   I like all animals, even spiders, but bats are my favourite.

2. Josh, who's very tall, helped me reach the book.
   Ama, my new friend, is coming over soon.
   Our house, the oldest on the street, makes strange noises.

3. Last Monday, which was very warm and sunny, we went to the beach. We travelled on a double-decker bus, which was orange, for over an hour. Ben, my best friend, fell asleep on the bus. Ben and I built a sculpture, a huge turtle, out of sand on the beach. Ella, who is very generous, let us eat some of her biscuits at lunchtime. When we got home, late that afternoon, we were tired but happy.

Now Try This:
E.g. The sun, bright red in the pink sky, was setting.
Dana, who drove lorries, was busy all morning.
Riley ate her meal, a lasagne, in complete silence.

Page 27 — Commas to Avoid Ambiguity

1. What time do you want to eat Fluffy? — Asking what time you want to eat Fluffy.
   What time do you want to eat, Fluffy? — Asking what time Fluffy wants to eat.

2. I bought chocolate, biscuits and cake.
   After watching, Olly, Ian and Paul went home.
   We decided to clean up, Rufus.
   Most of the time, travellers forget to bring a toothbrush.

3. Hubert liked cream, cakes and cherries.
   My best friends are Kiana, Albert and Doug.
   I invited my sisters, Patsy and Lizzie, for dinner.

4. In the first sentence, Ashley and Gwen are two different people. In the second sentence, 'Ashley' is Gwen's surname.

Page 28 — Brackets and Dashes

1. Jill (my cousin) has a pet snake.

2. Mrs Higgins (our next-door neighbour) has six cats.
   Hassan is going to the bookshop (the one near his house).
   Our Christmas party (the one at school) didn't go according to plan.

3. E.g. Percy (Amy's twin) lent me his bike.
   My friend (the one from America) moved to a new house.

4. My brother — who is in the army — is staying with us.
   Darla met a trapeze artist — Madame Volero — at the circus.
   Asa's kite — the bright red one — got stuck in a tree.

5. Hardi's house — the one with the green door — is very big.
   My aunt — who lives in Brighton — is coming to visit.

Page 29 — Single Dashes

1. I went for a run — I wanted to get fit.
   Simon told me his secret — he didn't like cheese.

2. I couldn't believe it — we saw a rare spotted wallaby.
   I needed some new socks — the old ones had holes in.
   Sean told his pig off — it had eaten all the pizza.

3. We were worried — we couldn't find our dog Lucky anywhere.
   I had that dream again last night — the one about pirates.
   Don't touch that button — you don't know what it does.
   Wen Yu climbed the tree — he wanted to see the view.

4. E.g. Mr Assad looked over the fence — he could see his neighbour's vegetable patch.
   We went into town — it was very busy.

Now Try This:
E.g. Because it separates two main clauses.

Page 30 — Hyphens and Bullet Points

1. blue-eyed sheep

2. My basketball-mad sister is always practising.
   Serena lives in a high-rise apartment building.

3. I had to re-mark the lines of the hockey pitch after it rained.
   Shana recapped the plot of the thriller for her mum.
   At school, we recycle all our scrap paper.
   I decided to return the new bike wheel when I realised it was bent.

Answers

4. You should have written a list of four instructions using bullet points correctly. If you started one bullet point with a capital letter you should have started every point with a capital letter. You could have put a full stop after every point or just the last point. E.g:
   - Cut out the shape you want your mask to be.
   - Decorate your mask using whatever materials you have.
   - Use a sharp pencil to make a hole on either side.
   - Thread elastic through the holes and tie a knot in each end.

Page 31 – Punctuating Speech

1. "Look where you're going!" my brother shouted as I tripped over his model.
   Tracey called to me, "Do you want to come over for tea tonight?"
   "It's the best present ever!" Jamal yelled excitedly.
   Jed asked me, "Can I go on your trampoline?"
   "I'll come too," said Polly, "since it was my idea."
   "Shall we watch TV?" Sam asked. "What do you want to do?"

2. "I can't find my toothbrush anywhere," Mum called.
   Olly said, "I think I'll go swimming tonight."
   "I'm sure I will find a cure for all illness," said Lauren.
   "I'm not sleepy," said Chris, "so I think I'll stay up longer."
   "Kell can't come," said Gemma, "but Nathan can."

3. E.g. Meg asked me, "Do you want a banana?"
   "Let's have some tea," said Jonah. "Get the teapot."

Now Try This:
E.g. "I never grow old," said Peter. "Isn't that great?"
"How will you get your driving licence?" asked Wendy.
"I suppose I hadn't thought about that," admitted Peter.

Pages 32-33 – Apostrophes

1. I'll, you're, it's
2. We walked Laura's dog.
3. I'm going home now.
   We're going to do what he says.
   I'd been expecting that it'd do that.
4. he will, you have, will not, could not
5. Peri would've enjoyed this if she had come.
   I didn't know you lived here.
   "Where's my pen?" asked Milo.
6. We're all going to Jamie's house for a sleepover.
   The glasses' rims were all chipped.
   Farah's tongue went blue after she ate the lolly.
   That drummer's hands are moving really quickly.
   Both farmers' pigs escaped that summer.
   The children's parents looked tired.
   The donkey's leg was really hairy.
7. E.g. Ellie's shirt was purple.
   The cat's tail is fluffy.
   The mouse's ear was twitching.
   The pandas' cubs played in the tree.
   The buses' tyres were flat.
8. The eagle spread its wings.
   I hope it's not too hot.
   I wonder if it's raining.
   The boat had lost its oars.
   Wow, it's really nice in here.
   This gum has lost its flavour.
   It's my birthday today.
   The cow curled around its calf.

Now Try This:
E.g. The bus was very hot because its air conditioning had broken. I couldn't believe how long the journey to Cornwall took, but it was worth it because it's beautiful. I borrowed Carla's camera to take photos.

Page 34 – Colons

1. I have lots of hobbies: reading, playing guitar, judo: and collecting shells.
   Zara didn't want: to go to the park: she had been there yesterday.
2. I'd like three things: a new bike, some chocolate and a time machine.
   I wish I could talk to animals: I'd like to know what my cat is thinking.
   The room was bright: all the lights were on.
3. Stan collected what he needed to paint a picture: paints, paper and brushes.
   Aisha went swimming: she needed to cool down.
   Aaron didn't want to go home: he was having too much fun.
   The otter could do tricks: diving, catching fish and waving.
   Caitlyn turned on the radio: she wanted to hear her favourite show.
   I took three things on holiday: my passport, some money and a book.
4. E.g. Chauncey was not having a great day: the wind had just stolen his hat.

Page 35 – Semi-Colons

1. My favourite subject is art and my least favourite is maths.
   Cora likes going to Iceland but I prefer Spain
2. In Paris, I want to visit the Louvre, a famous art gallery; the Eiffel Tower, the tallest structure in the city; and the shops, which are world-renowned.
   Nat was planning a special meal for Beth, including salmon, caught that day; peas, fresh from the garden; and tiramisu, Beth's favourite.
   During the summer, we went paddle boarding, which I've always wanted to try; sailing, which was fun; and paintballing, although I didn't like that.
3. We decided to go stargazing; Mel stayed at home. We saw the Milky Way, like a long white cloud; a meteor, which fell really fast; and Mars, which was a pinkish colour.

Now Try This:
E.g. Ezra likes dogs; Olu prefers rabbits.
I bought birdseed; my brother bought a birdbath.
Kit opened the box; it was empty.
Jan read a book; it was very short.

Pages 36-37 – Punctuation Practice

1. Do you want some melon?
   I think we should go for a walk.
   What a wonderful day!
   Shall I ask Carrie to come?
2. Last week, we saw fourteen ducklings.
   We decorated the table with candles, flowers and confetti.
   After Lee had ridden the dragon, he needed to sit down.
   Above Karen's head, a large flock of geese circled.
   I need to take the ingredients, an apron and my cookbook.
3. I looked under the bed — the treasure wasn't there.
   They — Nijay, Jimmy and Mo — went to the library.

Answers

4. I went to the book group to meet like-minded people.
   Kelsey gave her sister a hand-made birthday present.
   Frida Kahlo is my favourite twentieth-century artist.
   The robber left empty-handed after being chased by the owner's ferret.

5. You should have put a cross next to:
   Its not my fault that the crocodile escaped. — It's
   The three boy's sleeping bags lay on the floor. — boys'
   Mustafa is ill so well stay at home. — we'll
   You should've cut Callums' hair shorter. — Callum's

6. Genevieve made brownies; Huw ate them.
   That tree is going to fall down: the trunk is rotten.
   Sasha wants to go next door: they've got a new puppy.
   Abasi plays the cello well; I don't.
   Henry had three homes: London, Milan and Slough.

7. "I'm bored," said Cat, as she slowly leant back on the sofa.
   "Let's go and explore in the garden," suggested Sanav.
   "Okay," replied Cat. "It's got to be better than sitting around here."
   As they went outside, the sun came out and a rainbow lit the sky.
   "Look at that rainbow," said Sanav, "I bet there's a pot of gold at the end of this."
   "I'll race you," said Cat as she ran off.

Now Try This:
E.g. When they reached the end of the rainbow, there was a small pot sitting in an empty field.
"I can't believe it!" said Cat. "It's actually real!"
"Wait — there's only £5.50 in here!" yelled Sanav with disappointment.
"That's barely enough for two milkshakes," Cat said, bowing her head.

Pages 38-39 – Prefixes

1. False
2. two
3. trans-: transport, transmission, transplant
   semi-: semicircle
   tri-: triathlon, tripod
4. The council transformed the field into a new park.
   Rohan wants a new bicycle for his birthday.
   The school hockey team reached the semifinal of the tournament.
   Lisa speaks three languages. She's trilingual.
5. He cuts the cake into triangular slices.
   Band practice is biweekly — it happens on Tuesdays and Thursdays..
   The water was transparent — you could see to the bottom of the lake.
6. E.g. auto- means 'self'.
7. The team circumnavigated the globe in a tiny boat.
   The photocopier in the staff room has broken.
8. Salim took the rabbit to the vet to see if it had a microchip.
   The rocket needs to be aerodynamic so that it will fly well.
   The telephone rang loudly in the silent house.
9. My mum had to de-ice the car before we could leave.
   Tony was starting to re-evaluate his decision to join the circus.
   The pirate decided she had to co-operate with her enemies.

Now Try This:
E.g. resign and re-sign, remark and re-mark, repress and re-press, recreation and re-creation.

Page 40 – Words ending in 'shus' and 'shul'

1. residencial
2. suspicious, cautious, infectious, gracious
3. Tigers are very ferocious animals.
   Dani was usually shy, but she never felt self-conscious on stage.
   Andy is very conscientious about his work.
   Gertrude was a very obnoxious person.
4. special, initial, financial, glacial, confidential, partial, social, potential
5. The official spokesperson denied the alien sighting.
   This drink contains no artifical flavourings.
   My favourite film was a big commercial success.
   Meera is an influential member of our class.
   The latest games console costs a substantial amount of money.

Page 41 – Words ending in -ant and -ent

1. assistant, tolerant, argument
2. The museum was full of ancient dinosaur fossils.
   Alfie put on deodorant before he went out.
3. distant, accident
4. E.g. permanent — There is a permanent scratch on this mirror.
   elephant — The elephant performed a balancing trick.
   independent — Zoe had always been very independent.

Now Try This:
E.g. The flat's inhabitants were hesitant about moving.
Nazim had a talent for languages: he was fluent in five.

Page 42 – -ance, -ancy, -ence and -ency

1. arrogance
2. The strict teacher demanded obedience from all his pupils.
   I'm not convinced about my sister's innocence — I think she ate the cake.
   There was a sense of urgency about the search for the missing kangaroo.
   The decision to knock down the house was met with resistance.
   Can you please explain your absence from school last week?
3. science, infancy, balance
4. You should have circled: vacency, nuisence, consistancy.
   The correct spellings are: vacancy, nuisance, consistency.

Page 43 – -able, -ible, -ably and -ibly

1. comfortable, responsible, edible, miserable
2. considerably, visibly, audibly
3. Our dog has a very recognisable tail.
   The football supporters are remarkably loud today.
   Jenny has a hat that will turn you invisible!
   We had to dress sensibly for the hike.
   You sent me a letter, but your writing wasn't legible.
4. The game of hide-and-seek went terribly — I got stuck in the shed.
   Chidozie always wore very fashionable clothes.
   My uncle baked a cake for my birthday. It was irresistible.
   Tammi handled the problem very capably.

Now Try This:
E.g. likeable, usable, notably, valuably, invincible, eligible, impossibly, accessibly

Answers

Page 44 – Adding Suffixes to Words Ending in -fer

1. -ence
2. E.g. -ed, -ing, -al, -able
3. referred, referring, referral
4. You should have underlined: bufferring, referrence, prefered, sufferring, differred.
   The correct spellings are: buffering, reference, preferred, suffering, differed.
5. defer, confer

Page 45 – 'ei' and 'ie' Words

1. t<u>ie</u>r, forf<u>ei</u>t, y<u>ie</u>ld, th<u>ie</u>f, rel<u>ie</u>f, h<u>ei</u>st, n<u>ei</u>ther, l<u>ei</u>sure
2. w<u>ei</u>ght, r<u>ei</u>ndeer, sh<u>ie</u>ld
3. seize, weird, science
4. I can't believe my sunflower has reached a height of 200 cm.
   We stopped briefly on our way through the fields.
   They offer a variety of soups with either bread or crisps.

Now Try This:
E.g. deceive, society, freight, lies, mischief, perceive, siege, friendship, fiercely, receipt

Page 46 – Words with 'ough' in

1. 'off'
2. 'or' words — fought, ought, thoughtful, nought, bought
   'uff' words — enough, tough, roughly
3. though, doughy
4. She went to riding classes <u>throughout</u> the summer.
   Jonah bought a new <u>plough</u> for the farm.
   Helena <u>brought</u> a present and some balloons to the party.
   After the <u>drought</u>, the villagers were glad to see rain.
   Next year, we're moving to a different <u>borough</u> of Greater Manchester.

Page 47 – Words with Silent Letters

1. One of my dads is a secretary and the other is a <u>builder</u>.
   Lisa has drawn a new <u>design</u> for her rocket.
   The national flower of Scotland is a <u>thistle</u>.
2. You should have ticked: knight, autumn, written, could.
   You should have written: <u>g</u>narly, as<u>c</u>end, <u>g</u>uarantee, <u>h</u>ourly, thum<u>b</u>.
3. Samia beat a steady r<u>h</u>ythm on the drums.
   The best biscuits were all hidden in the back of the cup<u>b</u>oard.
   The <u>g</u>uard chased the thief through the museum.
   Bao got a <u>k</u>nitted jumper from his grandparents every birthday.

Now Try This:
E.g. <u>h</u>onour, <u>k</u>now, <u>w</u>rinkled, sa<u>l</u>mon, debu<u>t</u>, su<u>b</u>tle

Page 48 – Confusing Nouns and Verbs

1. naming words
2. Nouns — licence, prophecy, device
   Verbs — license, prophesy, devise
3. Can I ask you for some <u>advice</u> about this problem?
   Harvinder tries to <u>practise</u> his magic tricks every day.
   They will <u>advise</u> you to eat more fruit and vegetables.
   Kylie has had a lot of <u>practice</u> flying kites.
4. The band practi<u>se</u> their new songs every day after school.
   My neighbour has invented an amazing devi<u>ce</u> that toasts bread in five seconds.
   The council will licen<u>se</u> you to organise a street party this summer.
   Don't forget that we have hockey practi<u>ce</u> after school today.
   Joanna is very forgetful — she didn't bring her driving licen<u>ce</u> or her passport.

Page 49 – Homophones

1. The giraffe was so tiny that it only came up to her <u>waist</u>.
   My sister stayed in the <u>bridal</u> suite before her wedding.
   Ron thought the competition was a <u>waste</u> of time.
   This pumpkin is the biggest one that I have ever <u>grown</u>.
   Ibrahim needed a new <u>bridle</u> for his horse.
   She let out a <u>groan</u> when she saw the score.
2. A thick <u>mist</u> descended on the village.
   Abigail has always wanted to <u>write</u> a novel.
   Why do you eat <u>cereal</u> every morning for breakfast?
   The <u>ascent</u> to the top of the mountain was difficult.
   My grandfather made a big <u>profit</u> selling ice creams.
3. To employ someone. — hire
   Further above something. — higher
   To look for a short time. — peek
   The best or highest point. — peak

Now Try This:
draft — draught
medal — meddle
principle — principal
weather — whether
sent — scent or cent
compliment — complement

Pages 50-51 – Spelling Practice

1. I watched te<u>le</u>vision during the tr<u>ans</u>atlantic flight.
2. My friend has an ado<u>rable</u> hamster and two goldfish.
   The traffic jam made us unbear<u>ably</u> late for the concert.
   Yoga is a type of exercise that helps you become more flex<u>ible</u>.
3. weild, riegn, deisel, consceince, neice
4. The boxer won without knocking his opponent uncons<u>cious</u>.
   Jade loved all sports, but mar<u>tial</u> arts were her favourite.
   The laboratory was full of dangerous chemicals and no<u>xious</u> fumes.
5. mus<u>c</u>le, <u>w</u>hine, ha<u>l</u>ved, <u>h</u>onesty, g<u>u</u>itar, dou<u>b</u>t
6. cough, thought, doughnut
7. I tried to help my dad clean, but he said I was being a <u>hindrance</u>.
   Jack has a <u>tendency</u> to talk a lot when he feels nervous.
8. -ant — elegant, vacant, hesitant
   -ent — obedient, innocent, present
9. There was a rather unusual <u>guest</u> at the hotel this week.
   We visited the countryside for some <u>peace</u> and quiet.
   Sonali wanted some <u>assistance</u> with choosing the right pet.
10. preference, deferred, conferring, transferable
11. The correct spelling is: co-own.
    E.g. My mum and my uncle co-own the business.

Now Try This:
E.g. microchip, microwave, aeroplane, aerosol, semicircle, semitone, circumference, circumnavigate, tricycle, triangle

Answers

Pages 52-55 – Progress Test 1

1. aeroplane, televise, photocopy, circumstance
   (1 mark for each correct answer)
2. E.g. Next year I'm planning to:
   - visit my cousins
   - act in a play
   - go to the park
   (1 mark for each correct answer)
3. Kweku tripped over and injured his heel last night.
   That field used to be the site of the old castle.
   Is it possible to alter the size of this shirt?
   The special effects in this TV series are amazing.
   (1 mark for each correct answer)
4. precious, ambitious *(1 mark for each correct answer)*
5. Out of the two scooters, he said that he prefers this one here.
   Grace wants to buy a new jumper to replace her old one.
   I looked everywhere for that shoe after you lost it yesterday.
   (1 mark for each correct answer)
6. We went to the shops — we needed more milk.
   The llama — who was called Sid — was very friendly.
   (1 mark for each correct answer)
7. I grow fruit in my garden: apples, strawberries and oranges.
   Tyson works as a florist; Jenny is a firefighter.
   Hockey practice was cancelled tonight: it was raining too heavily. *(1 mark for each correct answer)*
8. Marie has driven two hundred miles to be here.
   I have never seen that painting before.
   Ezra has written a poem. *(1 mark for each correct answer)*
9. I shouldn't have taken the dog's toy — that one is its favourite. *(1 mark for each correct answer)*
10. She wants to buy those ones over there.
    Martin and I went to the woods to collect pine cones.
    Aren't you supposed to be at drama club tonight?
    They were winning the game of paintball.
    This new robot toy was already broken when I opened it.
    (1 mark for each correct answer)
11. E.g. Every Wednesday, I walk my pet squirrel.
    Shouting loudly, Tess ran away.
    In the field, there are twenty-two sheep.
    (1 mark for each correct answer)
12. E.g. Jamie was playing basketball after school.
    Li was ice-skating very gracefully.
    (1 mark for each correct answer)
13. It is important that you be quiet during the announcement. *(1 mark)*
14. "I think I'm going to the cinema tomorrow," said Bilan.
    Val whispered, "Let's keep this a secret until the party."
    "I saw two elephants," said Alfie, "and a tiger as well."
    (1 mark for each sentence that is punctuated correctly)
15. A brand new motorbike was bought by Rosie.
    Concert tickets were bought by us.
    (1 mark for each correct answer)
16. You should have circled:
    My best freind Aisha is very irresponsable. Last week, we went on a residencial trip to the Peak District with school. She got bored waiting for the safety demonstration to end and tried to clime a mountain by herself. If she'd been more patient, she wouldn't have been in trouble!
    You should have written:
    friend, irresponsible, residential, climb, patient
    (1 mark for circling the incorrect spelling and writing the correct spelling)

Pages 56-57 – The Titanic

1. "embarked"
2. E.g. There were "state-of-the-art facilities" on board.
3. "swift speed"
4. E.g. No. The text describes the iceberg's shape as "dim", which suggests that it was hard to see.
5. E.g. It makes the iceberg seem large and dangerous.
6. E.g. They would have been shocked. Many people thought it was "nearly impossible" for the *Titanic* to sink, so this news would have taken them by surprise.

Now Try This:
Any sensible improvements. For example:
- Stronger materials could have been used to build the ship so that it wouldn't have "ripped" as easily.
- There could have been rules about how fast the ship was allowed to travel when there were "icebergs in the vicinity".

Pages 58-59 – Letter by Serena Williams

1. fight
2. E.g. A family that "supported" her dream.
3. E.g. strength
4. her race and her gender
5. determined
6. E.g. Williams says that men and women in sport do "the same work", so they should be paid equally.
7. E.g. Williams hopes that women will share their stories of success, and that this will inspire even more women to follow their dreams.

Now Try This:
E.g. The letter inspires the reader. By saying she is "sure" the reader also had a dream, Williams encourages them to think about what they wanted to achieve when they were younger. Reading about Williams achieving her dream might then inspire the reader to pursue their own goals.

Pages 60-61 – A Connecticut Yankee in King Arthur's Court

1. "projecting"
2. "silk trappings that hung down all around him like a bedquilt"
3. personification
4. Hank is taken prisoner by the knight. — 3
   Hank wakes up in an unfamiliar place. — 1
   Hank climbse up a tree. — 2
5. E.g. The knight will take Hank to Camelot because Hank is now the knight's "property". Hank will realise that he has gone back in time after seeing more "old-time" armour, buildings and items. Hank will escape from the knight's custody and return to the present day.

Now Try This:
Any suitable answer. For example:
The image of "a vast grey fortress" creates the impression that Camelot has an intimidating castle, which could make the reader wonder about its history and who lives there.

Pages 62-63 – Poems about the Battle of Britain

1. E.g. early morning
2. E.g. It suggests that the pilot is completely focused on responding to the air raid sirens.

Answers

3. E.g. To show how fast the pilot is travelling.
4. E.g. *The Battle of Britain* is more exciting. There is a sense of urgency as the pilot's actions are "Frantic" and the danger remains a "mystery".
5. E.g. It emphasises how sharp and sudden the sound of the planes is.
6. E.g. Comparing the planes to the stones implies that the planes are in danger because they will also sink "to watery graves" if they are shot down.

Now Try This:
Any suitable answer. For example:
On Dover Beach. I enjoyed the use of positive and negative imagery, such as the stones that "dance" before "sinking".

Pages 64-65 – The Shapeshifter: Running the Risk

1. frantic
2. The hunting hounds will struggle to follow his scent if he runs through water.
3. E.g. powered
4. E.g. Owen's voice is familiar to Dax.
5. E.g. They show Dax's panicky struggle to breathe properly.
6. E.g. It makes him feel relieved. He "didn't pause" before going as "deep" into the hole as he could, which shows how glad he was to have found it.

Now Try This:
Any suitable answer. For example:
Yes. Dax takes risks throughout the extract, such as running through a stream in which he could "sink" and drown.

Pages 66-67 – The Pool

1. every two lines rhyme
2. E.g. "The oak is a mast in the ship of shade"
   "the beaming fat lady sun"
3. E.g. It suggests that the sun magically creates "fun" for people to enjoy.
4. E.g. They walk through a cornfield, climb over barbed wire, follow a stream and jump into a pool before returning to the car.
5. E.g. an exciting mood and a tired mood
   In lines 9-12, an exciting mood is created by dramatic verbs and adverbs such as "Hit", "froze" and "Suddenly".
   In lines 23-26, a tired mood is created by adverbs like "Sleepily" and the peaceful image of "rippling stars".

Now Try This:
Any suitable answer. For example:
Yes, I would like to go on a similar day out because the poem makes the trip sound magical. It describes the sun as a "Witch of warmth", which suggests that it is friendly

Pages 68-69 – Mary Shelley's Diary

1. it is too wet
2. E.g. bare or empty
3. E.g. It gives the reader an image of the mountain as a dangerous and uninviting place.
4. E.g. climbed
5. E.g. Mary writes that the evening was "calm and beautiful", which suggests that she prefers to travel then because it is peaceful.
6. "We saw Jura and the Lake like old friends."

7. E.g. Happy. Mary said that she "longed" to see her child, and when she finally gets to Chapuis they are reunited.

Now Try This:
Any suitable answer. For example:
No. Shelley's descriptions of "avalanches" and "torrents" of rain make the Alps sound like a very uninviting place.

Pages 70-71 – Interview with Quentin Blake

1. They think they're bad at it.
2. E.g. You've understood something.
3. brings them to life.
4. E.g. Yes. Blake says he built up a "good collaboration" with Dahl and that they had a similar sense of humour.
5. E.g. They are important but hard to draw. They need to attract readers without revealing lots of plot details.
6. E.g. A book's "flavour" could be a general idea of what a book is like.

Now Try This:
Any suitable answer. For example:
Blake seems like a kind and open-minded man. He says that he is "not fussy" about being asked to change his drawings, which suggests that he is willing to reach agreements with people.

Pages 72-73 – Who Needs Luck?

1. Any suitable feature, for example:
   - stage directions
   - character names on the left
2. E.g. Fred is surprised. He stutters when he gives his name to Miss Okeke.
3. "as sharp as a tack"
4. E.g. Yes, I think that Mr Sunday is a friendly man. He makes jokes during the interview and tells Fred to "call me Robert" instead of Mr Sunday.
5. E.g. He thinks that Fred isn't put off by the low pay.
6. E.g. No. He thinks Fred's salary and safety training are "trivialities", which suggests that he doesn't care about Fred very much.

Now Try This:
Any suitable answer. For example:
Yes. Fred moves "*awkwardly*" and is easily "*Bewildered*". This suggests that he lacks confidence in himself, so it is likely that he will be pressured into feeding the alligators at the zoo.

Pages 74-75 – Yorimasa and the Monster

1. It comes out at night
2. E.g. He was the only knight brave enough to face the monster.
3. his armour, a hunting-dress, a ceremonial cap
4. E.g. The writer uses the simile "the wind shrieked like a pack of wild demons" to describe the wind. This makes the weather sound threatening and implies that Yorimasa is in danger.
5. E.g. He only needs to use one arrow to kill the monster.
6. E.g. It gives the reader a clearer image of the monster's unnatural appearance, which makes it seem scarier.

Now Try This:
Any suitable answer. For example:
I think that Yorimasa will go on a new quest to fight other dangerous monsters because he is described as "brave" and has just been given a new sword.

Answers

Pages 76-77 — How to Cut a Pomegranate

1. free verse
2. "the heart. It will weep blood."
3. a metaphor
4. E.g. shiny
5. E.g. A child. The narrator's father uses commands like "Never". This shows authority and suggests that the narrator is a child being given instructions.
6. E.g. He might have felt disappointed. He told them to treat the fruit "with respect" and they "spurted" the juice out.

Now Try This:
Any suitable six-line stanza. For example:
Banana. Brown-flecked yellow skin
with sweet, soft flesh inside.
It makes me feel happy and healthy
when I devour one at lunchtime
and guilty, when I scatter one over ice cream.
Perfect, golden crescent moon.

Pages 78-79 — A Daughter of the Samurai

1. first-person narration
2. E.g. They mirror Sugimoto's fast movements and show how she is doing a lot of things quickly.
3. E.g. Everyone was weighed down by a feeling that something bad would happen.
4. E.g. She feels nervous. She bows "meekly" to her grandmother which suggests that she is worried.
5. E.g. Sugimoto's grandmother seems intimidating because she speaks "sternly" to Sugimoto.
6. E.g. Ishi helps Sugimoto treat Shiro, whereas her grandmother is very traditional and thinks being too generous to Shiro is "inappropriate."

Now Try This:
Any suitable answer. For example:
No. If I was reborn as someone's pet, I would depend on them for "good scraps" to eat.

Pages 80-83 — Progress Test 2

1. E.g. an impressive achievement
   (1 mark)
2. alliteration
   (1 mark)
3. Any two suitable features, for example:
   - an engaging headline
   - third-person
   - past tense
   - quotations
   (1 mark for each correct answer, up to 2 marks)
4. "who has since been exiled from the group"
   (1 mark)
5. E.g. She thinks it's a good indoor activity for families.
   (1 mark)
6. E.g. Jordan Poole. Wade Brook speaks "begrudgingly", whereas Jordan Poole offers more information and speaks in an interesting way. *(1 mark for a sensible answer, 1 mark for a sensible explanation)*
7. E.g. I think the Water Babies will try to build another secret water park because they have "a hatred of public swimming pools" and their current water park has been discovered.
   (1 mark for a sensible idea, 1 mark for a sensible explanation)
8. E.g. freezing — boiling   thoughtful — careless
   confident — timid   delicious — disgusting
   interesting — boring   orderly — chaotic
   (1 mark for each sensible antonym)
9. E.g. Shania walked her dogs around the park.
   Dominic paints pictures in art class.
   Ruth is climbing up the ladder.
   (1 mark for each sensible answer)
10. Manali hit the tennis ball.
    We will feed the llamas.
    (1 mark for each correct sentence)
11. Lucy entered the maze and soon became lost. She tried going left because the path looked promising, but it only led to a dead end. Retracing her steps didn't help, nor did trying to peep over the hedges. Eventually, after much searching, she found the exit.
    (1 mark for each correct answer)
12. Last week, the king, who is usually bad-tempered, invited everyone to his palace for a celebration. Surprised by his change of heart, I was suspicious and did not go.
    (1 mark for each correct comma)
13. I thought it would arrive early, but it was very last-minute. Her family-owned business had existed for a century.
    (1 mark for each correct answer)
14. They saw many sights: a waterfall, a cave and a forest. I chose to go kayaking; Harriet went swimming.
    (1 mark for each correct answer)
15. crucial, achieve, unpleasant
    (1 mark for each correct answer)
16. They sought the criminal.
    That horse tends to stare.
    (1 mark for each correct answer)

Page 84 — Planning Your Writing

1. If you're starting at university, you'll need to know how to cook. Otherwise, you may end up eating beans on toast every night. — Purpose: Advise
   Dad yawned loudly. Suddenly, the settee cushions clamped around him like a set of teeth. The settee was trying to eat Dad! — Purpose: Entertain
   Why use multiple utensils? Revolutionise how you eat with the all-new *Kniforkpoon*. A knife, a fork and a spoon all in one — buy yours now! — Purpose: Persuade
2. A letter from the mayor informing people about roadworks. — Formal, serious language, lots of information.
   A postcard to a family member telling them about a school trip. — Informal language, personal tone.
   A story about a pigeon who has to save the world. — Descriptive language, building suspense.
3. Any sensible order, for example:
   Earliest cars — 2
   Introduction — 1
   Conclusion — 5
   Cars improve — 3
   Electric cars — 4

Now Try This:
You should have considered how to organise the information in the story. For example:
- An opening that gives information about the cooking contest and who's taking part.
- A middle that says what people cook. Something could go wrong with one person's dishes.
- An ending that says who wins and why.

Answers

You should also have considered your audience. For example:
- The story might be set in a school and use some informal language.

Pages 85-86 – Editing Your Work

1. the text makes sense, sentences flow well together
2. You should have used the suggestions to improve the edited extract. Here are some examples of the types of changes you might have made:
   - Starting the story with action, e.g. 'Meera flicked through the TV channels, wishing that she had something more exciting to do.'
   - Describing the person who posted the package, e.g. 'A mysterious figure dressed head-to-toe in black floated down the drive like a ghost.'
   - Showing Meera's excitement, e.g. 'She tore open the package, her fingers as fast as lightning.'
3. You should have made suggestions to make the extract clearer and easier to read. Here are some parts of the extract that you could have suggested changing:
   - The first two sentences could be combined and/or rewritten to avoid repetition of 'Italy' and 'tower'.
   - The fourth and fifth sentences could be joined using a linking word or phrase (e.g. 'because' or 'since') to help the text flow. The second reference to 'tower' should be changed into a pronoun to prevent repetition.

Now Try This:
You should have written a letter complaining to the council and made sensible suggestions to improve your friend's work. Here are some suggestions you could have made:
- Split up the sentences to make it easier to read.
- Combine sentences to help the writing flow.
- Use paragraphs to group ideas together.

Page 87 – Proofreading Your Work

1. "Be<u>w</u>ear of th<u>ei</u>ves and pirates once you reach the port<u>?</u>" the captain yelled.
2. You should have identified and changed these mistakes:
   The spaceship cruised around the dusty, red planet for the third time that day. In the cockpit, several creatures were huddled around a tall woman <u>waring</u> (wearing) a navy flight helmet.
   <u>(")</u>Are you sure they landed on Mars, Commander<u>.(?)</u>" a wrinkly, blob-like creature at the back of the crowd <u>tenative</u> (tentatively) asked.
   "<u>Theyve</u> (They've) got to be here!" the woman <u>retorts</u> (retorted) through gritted teeth.
   On another day, she might <u>of</u> (have) made an example of the rude blob, but she had other things on her mind. She pulled up the visor on her helmet and began scanning the ground. A long, <u>tence</u> (tense) silence hung over the cockpit.
   "There! That's <u>there</u> (their) ship! Prepare for landing," the commander grinned, eager to finally catch the crooks who had stolen her laser goggles<u>_(.)</u>
   A siren wailed <u>as</u> (like) a banshee and the room was filled with a crimson red light. The creatures scrambled to <u>acsion</u> (action), pressing various switches and buttons before strapping <u>themselfs</u> (themselves) into their <u>seat's</u> (seats). <u>a</u> (A) mighty rumble came from behind them as the <u>endgines</u> (engines) fired up. The spaceship suddenly <u>begun</u> (began) accelerating <u>to wards</u> (towards) the planet, <u>bearly</u> (barely) allowing time for some creatures to put their seatbelts on.

Pages 88-89 – Magical Mystery Tours

1. To persuade customers
2.

Technique	Example from the extract	Effect of the technique
Repetition	you need Magical Mystery Tours! Let Magical Mystery Tours	Emphasises the name of the company and the tour.
List of three	Sun, sea and sand. **or** Mountains, moors and meadows	Makes it sound like there are lots of appealing locations.

3. Any suitable sentences. For example:
   Exaggeration — 'This adventure will absolutely change your life.'
   Rhetorical question — 'Do you like choosing your own routes?'
4. You should have rewritten the passage, using writing techniques to make it more persuasive. For example: 'Tired of the same old routine? Want to enjoy some sun or explore a hidden cave? Magical Mystery Tours has something perfect for customers of all ages. What's more, our trips are available from just £150, so the price is almost as magical as the journey!'
5. Any suitable advert that uses repetition, exaggeration, lists of three and rhetorical questions to persuade people to buy the product. For example:
   - Repetition — 'You always take your sunglasses away with you, now let your sunglasses take you away.'
   - Exaggeration — 'It's the most amazing invention!'
   - Lists of three — 'Travel beyond the moon, the stars and even outer space.'
   - Rhetorical questions — 'Do you wish you had magical sunglasses?'

Now Try This:
You should have written an advert for a toy or game, using language techniques to make your advert as persuasive as possible. For example:
- You could have made your chosen toy or game sound exciting using exaggeration, e.g. 'The fun never stops!'
- You could have used repetition to make your toy or game sound like it is enjoyable for a long time, e.g. 'Stretchy-Putty provides hours and hours of fun for all the family.'

Pages 90-91 – The Beautiful Game

1. <u>Lastly</u>, I would like to show you the photos of my cats and dogs.
2. The football World Cup is the biggest football tournament <u>in the world</u>. National teams play qualifiers each <u>year</u> to determine which teams will feature in the tournament, <u>usually</u> in the autumn and spring. The World Cup is traditionally held in the <u>summer</u> and lasts for <u>five weeks</u>.
3. You should have underlined:
   Just before the 1966 football World Cup was held in England, the Jules Rimet Trophy was stolen. <u>The Jules Rimet Trophy</u> was to be awarded to the World Cup winners. Pickles, a male collie cross, was walking with his owner one day when <u>Pickles</u> sniffed out the trophy! Pickles was already famous by the time that England won the World Cup that year and <u>Pickles</u> also went on to star in a film.
   You should have replaced all the words underlined above with pronouns to make the text flow better. For example:

Answers

Just before the 1966 football World Cup was held in England, the Jules Rimet Trophy was stolen. <u>This</u> was to be awarded to the World Cup winners. Pickles, a male collie cross, was walking with his owner one day when <u>he</u> sniffed out the trophy! Pickles was already famous by the time that England won the World Cup that year and <u>he</u> also went on to star in a film.

4. The Euros is another tournament played every four years, <u>although</u> only European countries take part. The Soviet Union won the first tournament in 1960, <u>when</u> it was hosted by France. The host country changes every tournament, <u>for example</u>, it was first held in England in 1996.
5. 'Dick, Kerr Ladies FC' were really popular.
6. Paragraph 1: a, c, h, e.
    Paragraph 2: d, b, f, g.

Now Try This:
You should have explained what your chosen machine does and how to use it. Here are some techniques you could have used:
- Pronouns, e.g. 'The vacuum cleaner was invented in 1901. It sucks up dust as you push it across the floor.'
- Linking words or phrases, e.g. 'However, vacuum cleaners have become much more affordable over time.'

Pages 92-93 – Blue Whales

1. Most children dislike Brussels sprouts.
2. False
3. Blue whales can be found in <u>nearly all</u> of the world's oceans. Some people think that there will soon be so many ships in the ocean that blue whales will <u>sometimes</u> find getting around difficult. Blue whales are <u>typically</u> solitary creatures but they <u>can be</u> found in pairs as well.
4. You should have underlined these opinions:
    'Blue whales are majestic creatures.'
    'sadly they are an endangered species.'
    'which is really sad'
    You should have rewritten the extract using only facts and an objective tone. For example:
    Blue whales are the largest mammal on Earth. Their hearts are the same size as a small car and their tongues can weigh as much as an elephant. Blue whales are an endangered species. There are only around 10 000 - 25 000 blue whales left in the wild.
5. Blue whales communicate using low-pitched sounds.
    — with each other
    Sound travels faster through water than air.
    — it travels through
    Other whales can hear the sounds but humans often can't. — hear the sounds
    Although it is the biggest, the blue whale is not the loudest.
    — animal on earth
6. You should have written a clear, objective report. Here are some techniques you could have used:
    - Generalisations, e.g. 'Blue whales tend to live for a long time in the wild.'
    - Technical terms, e.g. 'Blue whales can achieve a top speed of 30 miles per hour.'

Now Try This:
Your report should be clear and informative. Here are some techniques you could have used:
- Facts about your chosen topic, e.g. 'Rugby Union is played with two teams, with 15 players on each team.'
- Technical terms, e.g. 'Positions in rugby include the scrum-half, props and a hooker.'
- Generalisations, e.g. 'Rugby is followed by many people worldwide.'

Pages 94-95 – A King of the Past

1. You should have circled: The ruby and sapphire necklace.
    You should have underlined: which I bought
2. The Cooper family of Littlewick-on-Candle had their mealtime interrupted yesterday by a surprise guest. The man claimed to be the legendary British leader, King Arthur.
3. The first pair of sentence parts should be arranged like this:
    1. Before the family noticed, Arthur knighted the cat.
    2. Arthur knighted the cat before the family noticed.
    The next pair of sentence parts should be arranged like this:
    1. In a fit of rage, Arthur called the TV a witch.
    2. Arthur called the TV a witch in a fit of rage.
4. Any suitable relative clauses. For example:
    The king then explained that he hadn't had a nap in over a century, so he went to sleep on the family's sofa, <u>which was very small</u>.
    In the morning Benjamin, <u>who is eleven</u>, took the king to a cafe <u>that is popular with locals</u>. Eyewitnesses report that Arthur ate a small army of gingerbread men.
5. Any suitable rewriting of the sentences that includes relative clauses and varied sentence structures. For example:
    Arthur, <u>who had slept for nineteen hours</u>, rode the horse around the town. Arthur attacked the dragon statue, <u>which is twenty feet tall and made of plastic</u>.
6. Your writing should be clear and informative.
    Here are some techniques you could have used:
    - Noun phrases, e.g. '<u>The agitated king</u> was taken to <u>a small cell in the police station</u>.'
    - Relative clauses, e.g. 'The king, <u>who was impressed by the police officer's strength</u>, was heard asking Constable MacDonald if she wanted to serve as one of his knights.'

Now Try This:
Your writing should include noun phrases, relative clauses and varied sentence structures. For example:
- You could describe the unexpected visitor using an expanded noun phrase, e.g. '<u>The rain-soaked witch with the magic broomstick</u> dried herself off in the corridor.'
- You could use a variety of sentence structures to narrate an incident, e.g. 'The witch remained in the house for several hours. To the landlord's disbelief, she began making a potion in the kitchen.'

Pages 96-97 – Letter to a Youth Group

1. Your headteacher
2. Dear Mrs Evans,
    You recently sent a letter asking for new <u>stuff</u> that my daughter's youth group could do to benefit other people who live in this <u>neck of the woods</u>. My daughter and I had a <u>chinwag</u> and we were <u>chuffed</u> with our idea. We <u>reckon</u> the youth group could establish a dog-walking service. You could charge <u>a couple of quid</u> for people who live in the area, and also offer the service to the local dog shelter. <u>Kids</u> could go out in pairs to walk the dogs. I'm sure that most of your members would be <u>up</u> <u>for this</u>.

Answers

3. I <u>believe</u> that this service would be a <u>really</u> good addition to the group's activities for several reasons. Firstly, it would <u>encourage</u> young people's involvement in the community, which would improve the group's <u>reputation</u> in the area. I am also firmly convinced that this activity would be a <u>brilliant</u> chance for young people to <u>interact</u> with a wide range of different people. In my opinion, your members would be able to learn <u>a great deal</u> from others in the community if you decided to <u>commence</u> this dog-walking service.

4. Any suitable clauses. For example:
Secondly, a dog-walking service would require young people to care for animals, <u>teaching them responsibility</u>. If you were to connect the service with the local dog shelter, <u>which homes abandoned dogs</u>, the volunteers would also be helping to care for dogs that are in need of love and affection. This activity would be wonderful for everyone involved <u>because of these benefits</u>.

5. Any suitable ending which continues the first sentence and includes a sign-off. For example:
   Lastly, I think this service would be beneficial for young people's health. It would provide an enjoyable and exciting way for young people to increase the amount of exercise they do. Spending time with animals can also improve people's mental health, and this improvement will only be greater if the time is spent outdoors.
   Yours sincerely,
   Mrs Habeb

Now Try This:
Your letter should have at least three paragraphs and use formal language. Here are some techniques you could have used:
- A suitable opening, e.g. 'Dear Mr Piatek' or 'To whom it may concern'.
- Formal language, e.g. 'My family recently ordered a birthday cake from your business and it had an impressive appearance, which improved our celebrations.'
- A clear structure — you could write a paragraph on each reason for the bakery to donate a prize, e.g. 'If you donated a prize to the school, it would be a brilliant advertisement for your bakery.'

Pages 98-99 – The Dragon Rider

1. personification
2. You should have underlined these similes:
Bianca's eyes glinted like diamonds
as fierce and determined as a lion
You should have circled these metaphors:
Her smile was a crescent moon
Her stomach a twisted knot
Any suitable explanation of a simile or metaphor from the text. For example:
   - 'Her smile was a crescent moon' suggests Bianca felt happy about the day ahead.
   - 'as fierce and determined as a lion' shows that Bianca is brave.
3. 'Bianca's feet were wings as she flew through the silent forest.' — Metaphor
'Her hair streamed out behind her like a mighty knight's banner.' — Simile
'Branches waved as she ran through the trees, cheering her on in her quest.' — Personification
4. Any suitable appeals to the senses. For example:
She crept along the <u>gloomy</u> tunnel which led to the dragon's lair. The ground was <u>slippery</u>, and her hands grazed <u>jagged</u> rocks when she reached out to stop herself from falling. As she edged along the passage, the air became warmer. The scent of <u>smoke</u> in the air made her stifle a cough, and a <u>rumbling</u> noise told Bianca that the dragon was close.
5. Any suitable sentences that use personification to give the objects human qualities. For example:
   - 'Glittering coins <u>winked</u> at Bianca.'
   - 'A chest full of gold <u>stood proudly</u> in the corner.'
   - 'A fire <u>spat</u> sparks around the cave.'
6. You should have used similes, metaphors and appeals to the senses to describe Bianca and her flight. For example:
   - You could have used metaphors to describe Bianca's wonder, e.g. 'Her face was a picture of glee as the dragon twisted and turned in the air.'
   - You could have used similes to describe her actions, e.g. 'Bianca laughed like a hyena.'
   - You could have used appeals to the senses to describe her flight, e.g. 'She felt the wind in her hair and tasted salt on her tongue as they swooped down over the sea.'

Now Try This:
You should have written a description of each place. Here are some techniques you could have used:
- Similes, e.g. 'The witch's castle glowed like a beacon.'
- Appeals to the senses, e.g. 'The enormous lake was bright and dazzling in the sunshine.'
- Metaphors, e.g. 'The mountain was an impressive ice sculpture.'

Pages 100-101 – Far From Rome

1. The way it feels.
2.

Example	What atmosphere it creates
daring, exciting adventures	A thrilling atmosphere.
a dark and terrible omen	A tense atmosphere.

3. Icy, stabbed, perilously, slipping, prickled, nervous, rumbled, gulped, ominously, sinister.
4. Any suitable adjectives or adverbs which create a positive atmosphere. For example:
Justus had never felt so <u>grateful</u> to <u>finally</u> stop marching and sit down. He wiped his <u>sweaty</u> forehead and looked around. The sight of the tiny port gave his <u>exhausted</u> body a fresh burst of energy. A <u>warm</u> orange light blinked from the top of a lighthouse, guiding ships <u>safely</u> to the shore. The long, straight road that stretched out towards the <u>welcoming</u> town looked <u>familiar</u>. The place seemed to promise refuge, and Justus gave a <u>relaxed</u> smile. He would <u>happily</u> rest his head here tonight.
5. Any suitable rewriting of the extract. Here are some techniques you could have used:
   - Adjectives which create a mysterious atmosphere, e.g. 'The long, <u>winding</u> road that stretched out towards the <u>shadowy</u> town looked <u>intriguing</u>.'
   - Adverbs which create a mysterious atmosphere, e.g. 'A flickering orange light blinked <u>inexplicably</u> from the top of an abandoned lighthouse, <u>eerily</u> illuminating the shore.'
   - Verbs which create a mysterious atmosphere, e.g. 'He <u>shivered</u> in the dark and peered around.'

Now Try This:
Your writing should be descriptive and should create a tense atmosphere, while also advancing the story. For example:
- You could make the preparations seem rushed, e.g. 'The call to battle sounded so suddenly that Justus barely had time to grab his shield before dashing from his tent.'

Answers

- You could make the setting seem unsettling, e.g. 'A thick, terrible mist crept into the camp.'
- You could make Justus seem worried, e.g. 'Dread settled in Justus's stomach as he got dressed.'

Pages 102-103 – A Bumpy Ride

1. You should have underlined:
   Where's, can't, she'll
   You should have circled:
   Woah, gobsmacked

2.

Character	Example	What it shows
Hiro	"Yeah, I suppose,"	He feels nervous
Imogen	"I can't wait to get inside!"	She is excited

3. You should have circled one of the groups of options below to create a consistent atmosphere:
   To create a creepy atmosphere:
   no, eerie, busier, strange, nervously, graveyard.
   To create a lively atmosphere:
   so many, crowded, quieter, more excited, enthusiastically, party.

4. You should have rewritten the extract to include suitable dialogue which makes the important plot points clear. For example:
   - Imogen persuading Hiro to go on the enormous roller coaster, e.g. '"I've always wanted to go on that ride," Imogen told him. "They say it's the highest in England!"'
   - Hiro refusing to go on the ride and offering an alternative, e.g. '"There's no way I'm going on that," Hiro replied adamantly. He looked at the map. "What about that boat ride? That looks like fun."'
   - Imogen insisting on the ghost train instead, e.g. '"I want to go on something that's exciting. Oh, look!" she shouted, pointing. "How about the ghost train? We are definitely going on that!"'

5. You should have used dialogue to describe what Hiro and Imogen do next. Here are some techniques you could have used:
   - Developing the characters using dialogue, e.g. '"I'm sure that someone will be here to help us soon," said Imogen cheerfully. "In the meantime, let's tell each other jokes to keep our spirits up."' — this shows Imogen's kindness.
   - Setting a suitable and consistent atmosphere using dialogue, e.g. '"What was that noise? I'm sure I just heard something in the shadows," whispered Hiro, reaching for Imogen's hand.' — this creates a scary atmosphere.

Now Try This:
Your writing should include dialogue to create an exciting atmosphere, develop your characters, and advance the action. For example:
- You could use dialogue to show what the characters are like, e.g. 'Jimmy announced, "I promised my little sister that I'd buy her favourite chocolates for her."' — this shows that Jimmy is generous and thoughtful.
- You could create an exciting atmosphere using dialogue, e.g. '"Look at that!" Heather exclaimed. "It looks absolutely magical."'
- You could use dialogue to move the plot forward, e.g. '"I wonder what's in this room," said Jimmy. "The tour guide isn't looking. Quick, let's sneak in and find out!"'

Pages 104-105 – Beneath the Stones

1. 3 — The bird lays eggs.
   1 — The bird hatches.
   2 — The bird grows up.

2. B, E, D, C, A.

3. Any suitable explanation of why the writer included the flashback. For example:
   - The contrast between the sunny woods and the dark tunnel emphasises Alexis's regret.
   - The calm nature of the flashback heightens the tension of Alexis's current situation.
   - The sunny depiction of nature suggests that there is something wonderful and magical about the map.
   - The flashback makes the reader more curious about how Alexis found the map.

4.

Cliffhanger	How it makes you feel
Suddenly, he heard footsteps padding softly behind him.	It makes me feel nervous.

5. Your ending should include a cliffhanger and a flashback. Here are some elements you could have included:
   - A flashback to create doubt/suspicion about Malachi's character, e.g. 'Malachi was talking about growing up in the countryside. Alexis suddenly remembered Malachi's words from the previous night: "I've lived down here all my life." Which was true? Was Malachi lying to him?'
   - A cliffhanger to create tension, e.g. 'As Alexis sat down on the coach, he had a strange feeling. He could feel the eyes of all the other passengers on him, as if they knew about the treasure in his rucksack. As the coach doors closed, the driver switched off the engine, stood up and strode slowly towards Alexis.'

Now Try This:
Your writing should have a varied structure and it should include a cliffhanger. For example:
- Your story could be told in a non-chronological order, e.g. the story could start in the middle of Alexis's next adventure, before including a flashback to show how he found the missing section of the map.
- You could end your third paragraph with a cliffhanger, e.g. 'He couldn't believe it: he had found the chest containing the missing portion of the map. He opened it up and saw a scrap of parchment, smaller than he expected. With trembling fingers, he unrolled it and read the words: "You lose, Alexis — I was here first."'

Pages 106-107 – The Animals of the Rainforest

1. boat, float, wrote

2. You should have underlined:
   grin and grow; fireflies flicker; it scrunches its simple, smiling face; pitiful pace; tallest of trees; reaches the roots

3. Any suitable alliterative words. For example:
   The jaguar <u>stealthily</u> stalks its prey,
   But <u>brave</u> Benjamin scares it away.
   Squirrel monkeys <u>strut</u> and swing,
   They <u>look</u> and laugh at everything.
   The <u>tremendous</u> toucan glides through the clouds,
   Then chirps a <u>cheerful</u> song out loud.

4. Any suitable imagery. For example:
   The frog's skin was as orange as <u>the setting sun</u>.
   The snake coiled around the branch like <u>a vine</u>.

Answers

The boar was <u>a bullet, zooming across the jungle</u> <u>floor</u>.
The waterfall roared as loudly as <u>a jet plane</u>.

5. You should have circled: buzzes, rumbles, flapping.
   Your poem should use onomatopoeic words to create a busy atmosphere. For example:
   - You could describe the sounds of nature, e.g. the <u>creaking</u> of tree trunks or the <u>howling</u> of the wind.
   - You could describe the sounds that animals make, e.g. the <u>growling</u> of tigers.

6. You should have underlined: blue, do
   Your poem should have the same number of beats per line as the original and the same rhyme scheme (the second and fourth lines should rhyme — that is, it should have an ABCB rhyme scheme). For example:
   Against the sky, a butterfly, (8 beats)
   Gently flutters from here to <u>there</u>, (8 beats)
   My heart cries out, "I wish that were me! (9 beats)
   I'd love to float up through the <u>air</u>." (8 beats)

Now Try This:
Your poems should each have a different rhyme scheme and rhythm. For example:
- You could rhyme each line of your poem and give it a regular rhythm, e.g.
  The turtles show off their shiny <u>shell</u>,
  And ride the tide like a <u>carousel</u>.
- Alternatively, you could use free verse, with no regular rhythm or rhyme scheme.

Pages 108-113 – End of Year Test

1. E.g. The author says that Tom wants to "make no sound" when he opens the door. He doesn't want anyone to hear him, which suggests that he shouldn't be going outside.
   (1 mark for a sensible answer, 1 mark for a sensible explanation)

2. personification *(1 mark)*

3. anger *(1 mark)*

4. "steal" *(1 mark)*

5. run across the grass, jump over the flower-beds, look inside the greenhouse, go inside the greenhouse, walk through the trees, climb the trees, hide from people.
   (1 mark for each correct activity, up to 2 marks)

6. E.g. Yes. The descriptions of the "glittering" greenhouse windows and the "richness" of the greenery make the garden seem beautiful. *(1 mark for a sensible answer, 1 mark for a sensible explanation)*

7. E.g. Tom is mischievous. He says that if people "came calling him" he would ignore them and "hide" in the trees. *(1 mark for a sensible answer, 1 mark for a sensible explanation)*

8. You should have circled:
   Mia goes swimming
   wishes can come true
   we enjoy biking
   You should have underlined:
   the tree over there
   little slimy snails
   those fluffy clouds
   (1 mark for each correct answer)

9. E.g. Nico's scarf is red.
   The bat's cavern was dark.
   My giraffes's spots vanished!
   (1 mark for each sensible sentence)

10. The <u>sole</u> of my shoe made a pattern in the snow.
    Many kings have sat on that grand, golden <u>throne</u>.
    The old man told us an exciting <u>tale</u> about a brave warrior.
    (1 mark for each correct answer)

11. <u>The bedroom</u> was decorated. — P, subject
    The snake shed its <u>skin</u>. — A, object
    (1 mark for each correct sentence)

12. I bought three flavours of ice cream<u>:</u> toffee, mint and vanilla.
    Before I could eat it<u>,</u> a seagull, which was hungry<u>,</u> stole it.
    Feeling annoyed<u>,</u> I shouted loudly<u>,</u> "Buy your own you greedy bird<u>!"</u>
    (1 mark for each correctly punctuated sentence)

13. E.g. Elise and Imran tiptoed <u>quietly</u> into the haunted house. They could dimly make out a <u>narrow</u> staircase and spiders studying them <u>curiously</u> from the roof, some dangling down on cobwebs. "This is <u>spooky</u>," whispered Imran, looking <u>nervously</u> at Elise.
    (1 mark for each sensible word)

14. You should have ticked:
    Mariko is cartwheeling.
    They are climbing a tree.
    (1 mark for each correct answer)
    You should have written:
    Mariko was cartwheeling.
    They were climbing a tree.
    (1 mark for each correct answer)

15. beneficial, important, probably, emergency
    (1 mark for each correct answer)

16. Millions of years ago, dinosaurs roamed the Earth. <u>However</u>, these creatures went extinct. A large crater has been discovered, <u>so</u> some scientists believe the dinosaurs were killed by a meteor, <u>whereas</u> others think their extinction was caused by a volcanic eruption.
    (1 mark for each correct answer)

17. E.g. When Katie saw the carefully wrapped box, she <u>leapt</u> out of her chair. <u>Eagerly</u>, she tore the paper off the present and opened the lid. When she looked inside and saw the box's <u>spectacular</u> contents, she <u>squealed</u>. "A scooter!" she cried <u>loudly</u>. "I can't believe it!"
    (1 mark for each sensible word)

18. E.g. The blanket was as soft as a bird's feather.
    The star was a burning arrow shooting across the sky.
    The rough wind knotted my smooth hair.
    (1 mark for each sensible sentence)

19. E.g. Climbing Mount Everest is difficult.
    Spider monkeys can grab things with their tails.
    (1 mark for each correct sentence)

20. E.g. Paula's shoulders relaxed. To her relief, the creature seemed relatively harmless. She went to take a step closer to it, then froze. The creature's pleasant smile was becoming a snarl. *(1 mark for any sensible ending, 1 mark for including a cliffhanger)*

21. You should have underlined:
    Jittery Jim, without warning, slid and slipped
    You should have circled:
    clipped, splash
    (1 mark for each correct answer)
    You should have written two more lines that share a rhyming word at the end and have nine beats each. E.g. 'But to his surprise, Jim was not sad.
        "Drop me back in — the water's not bad!"'
    (1 mark for using the same rhyme scheme, 1 mark for using the same number of beats per line)